Financing Prosperity by Dealing with Debt

GLOBAL PROSPERITY IN THOUGHT AND PRACTICE

Series Editors:
Christopher Harker
Yuan He
Henrietta Moore

Global Prosperity in Thought and Practice draws together research that rethinks what prosperity means for people around the globe. Contributions challenge the prevailing understanding of prosperity by developing alternative models and ways of thinking; presenting robust empirical evidence, innovative policies and emerging technologies for securing prosperity; and starting compelling public discussions about how we can flourish in the future.

Financing Prosperity by Dealing with Debt

Edited by Christopher Harker and Amy Horton

First published in 2022 by
UCL Press
University College London
Gower Street
London WC1E 6BT

Available to download free: www.uclpress.co.uk

ISBN: 978-1-80008-189-5 (Hbk.)
ISBN: 978-1-80008-188-8 (Pbk.)
ISBN: 978-1-80008-187-1 (PDF)
ISBN: 978-1-80008-190-1 (epub)
DOI: https://doi.org/10.14324/111.9781800081871

Contents

Part III Retaking the economy

List of figures and tables

List of contributors

Jerry During is the chief executive officer and co-founder of Money Advice and Education.

Daniel Edelstyn is a filmmaker and co-creator of the Hoe Street Central Bank.

Martin Groombridge is chief executive officer of London Capital Credit Union, which can claim to be the UK's oldest credit union.

Christopher Harker is an associate professor at the Institute for Global Prosperity, UCL.

Amy Horton is a lecturer in economic geography in the Department of Geography, UCL.

Charlotte Johnson is a senior research fellow at the Institute for Sustainable Resources, UCL.

Fanny Malinen is a member of the Research for Action workers' collective, which produces research to support social, economic and environmental justice.

Nathan Mladin is senior researcher at Theos think tank, which stimulates debate about the place of religion in society through research, commentary and events.

Johnna Montgomerie is a professor of international political economy in the Department of European & International Studies at King's College London.

Hilary Powell is an artist and co-creator of the Hoe Street Central Bank.

Josh Ryan-Collins is a senior research fellow at the Institute for Innovation and Public Purpose, UCL.

Joseph Spooner is an assistant professor in the Department of Law, London School of Economics and Political Science.

Acknowledgements

The editors would like to thank all of the contributors to this volume for their hard work during a very difficult period of time.

We would also like to recognise the contribution made by all participants at the 2019 Financing Prosperity by Dealing with Debts symposium, where many of the chapters were first presented.

Many thanks to Yuan He for feedback on the initial book proposal and Chris Penfold for his editorial guidance and support throughout the submission and review process.

Chapter authors would like to collectively thank all the people who provided feedback on earlier drafts of their work.

1

Introduction: Financing prosperity by dealing with debt

Christopher Harker

This book asks – and begins to answer – some vital questions about how we finance real prosperity. The Covid-19 pandemic has seen global debt levels rise to record levels (Strohecker 2021). Even before the pandemic began, we faced historically high and rising levels of indebtedness across the globe (Han, Medas and Yang 2021). Such indebtedness is created because in too many places our current political and economic systems have created conditions in which people can only afford to survive and thrive – securing housing, energy, access to transportation, health care and education – through credit (Graeber 2011; Lazzarato 2012, 2015). These systems are also undermining the very habitability of our planet (Raworth 2017). If we want to create more inclusive, sustainable and equitable societies, among the first things we need to develop are solutions for enduring problematic forms of debt. This will involve creating and proliferating alternatives for those most in need, while transforming the structures, institutions and practices that are responsible for producing our current heavily indebted societies. Such transformations will also need to address problems such as the planetary climate emergency and populist politics if they are to contribute to truly inclusive and sustainable prosperity.

Borrowing money is bound up not only with survival but also with people's aspirations for a better future for themselves, their families and their communities (James 2015). Therefore, dealing with debt must be thought about in relation to the broader question of how to create systems, institutions, infrastructures and practices that allow people and communities to finance the lives *they* want to live. How can we enable a large majority, rather than a small minority, of people to create lives based on what matters to them? How, in other words, can we create pathways to prosperity, where prosperity is understood as geographically, historically and socially diverse ideas about what it means to live well? Transnational comparative research conducted by the UCL Institute for Global Prosperity suggests that across this diversity there are some common threads (Moore and Mintchev 2021). Routes to greater global prosperity will involve fighting inequality, promoting social cohesion, safeguarding the environment, providing education, health and decent employment and giving people hope for the future (Moore 2015). The good news is that there are already many innovative ideas and practices through which institutions and multiple publics are transforming lives and livelihoods (Gibson-Graham, Cameron and Healy 2013). While we seek to learn from all these innovations wherever they might be, this book focuses on those that address debt and finance in the UK. To contextualise them, this introductory chapter begins by outlining the scope of current debt problems. This discussion is then followed by a section that outlines how the Financing Prosperity Network (FPN) uses cross-disciplinary methods to bring together academic, practitioner, activist and policy communities to work towards solutions. The final section previews the chapters in the rest of the book, which are organised into three sections, each offering a different approach to financing prosperity by dealing with debt. Chapters in the first section, **rethinking debt obligations**, unpack the moral and social basis of present debt-fuelled economies, challenging the validity of many contemporary forms and modes of debt. In the second section, **rewriting the rules**, authors foreground legal and political methods for changing the rules of the system, to provide debt relief to those who most need it and reshape national and household economies for more inclusive and sustainable flourishing. The third and final section, **reworking community economies**, focuses on how community-led initiatives are taking matters into their own hands and generating grassroots solutions to the problems of debt and finance. A concluding chapter draws out some of the interconnections between the three sections and examines alternatives to debt financing for a 'just transition' to sustainable, caring economies.

While this book was conceived and partly written before the onset of the Covid-19 pandemic, that has only made addressing debt more urgent. Drawing on hard-won insights from extensive research, lived experience and ongoing struggles, the volume offers a broad range of innovative ideas that will help academics, practitioners, activists and policymakers across the UK and beyond as they seek to remake better post-Covid worlds. Authors have written in an accessible manner, avoiding jargon wherever possible, to enable multiple audiences to engage with the arguments and narratives of change offered. Collectively, our key argument and contribution is to foreground a novel understanding of prosperity – as what people themselves value – to guide the reorganisation of political, social and economic systems so that such systems work for all people and the entire planet.

Problems of debt

Since the financial crisis of 2008, multiple kinds of debt crisis have impacted people living in the UK, and initial evidence suggests these have been accentuated by the policy response to the Covid-19 pandemic (Harker, Huq and Charalambous 2020). Debt has been a particularly acute problem since the onset of austerity politics. Following the 2008 financial crisis, successive UK governments (like their European counterparts) cut spending on public services to pay down a public debt burden – incurred by bailing out failing banks – that was deemed to have become too large (Blyth 2013; Langley 2014). The narrative that the government must pay its debts relies on the idea that government borrowing is similar to household borrowing, and thus the state must pay (back) what it owes. This equation of the state finances with private household finance has been heavily contested, since it ignores significant differences between the two, not least the ability of states to create their own money through central banks (Blakeley 2019). Austerity has caused hardship for the poorest in society and done little to enable economic recovery. The failure of austerity economics is more widely recognised in emerging responses to the Covid-19 recovery, as massive levels of government borrowing – the UK's national debt reached £2 trillion in July 2020 (Inman and Wearden 2020) – have been necessary once again to protect the nation's physical and economic health. Even institutions like the International Monetary Fund (IMF) argue that post-Covid austerity is neither necessary (Giles 2020) nor advisable (Chamon and Ostry 2021) in an era of record-low interest rates.

The drive to reduce state debt through public service retrenchment has directly caused rapid rises in levels of personal debt (Gardner, Gray and Moser 2020). People who had previously relied on various forms of social transfers and workers whose wages stagnated turned to credit to get by. The scale of this growth has been eye-watering. Between 2013 and 2019, personal debt grew six times faster than wages, taking inflation into account (Jubilee Debt Campaign 2019). During the period 2012–17, unsecured credit increased 19 per cent, car finance doubled, student debt doubled to £100 billion and council tax arrears increased 12 per cent (Inman and Barr 2017). By 2019, Britons owed a total of £72.5 billion on credit cards, an amount 24 per cent greater than on the eve of the 2008 financial crash (Chapman 2019). At the start of 2020, the Trades Union Congress (2020) reported that the average UK unsecured household debt stood at a record £14,540. But the distribution of this debt is uneven, both socially and geographically: 'The ONS's Wealth and Assets Survey [WAS] . . . shows that households in the lowest wealth decile are almost twice as likely as those in the highest wealth decile to have financial debt'[1] (Trades Union Congress 2020). Geographically, this dataset shows that 22 per cent of adults living in London reported their debt was 'a heavy burden', compared with 8 per cent of adults living in Scotland (Office for National Statistics 2019). Data about the number of county court judgements – a key publicly accessible record for gauging problem debt – indicates that 'personal debt is a particular problem in cities and large towns in Wales and the North of England', where pay is low and higher numbers of people receive state benefits (Narayan 2020, 3). During the UK Covid-19 lockdowns, while better off households were able to pay off debts, lower-income households fell behind on repayments and were driven to borrow even more, often to pay for basics like rent, energy bills and council tax (StepChange 2020a). Such changes take place amid a rise in secured forms of credit, as declining housing affordability has spurred growing levels of residential mortgage debt – a total of £1,486 billion by late 2019 (Financial Conduct Authority 2019). Thus, while it is true to say that the UK is a heavily indebted nation, this is nuanced terrain, full of social and spatial difference. Nationwide solutions to debt will need to be aligned with local-scale responses and actions that account for the specificity of debt problems.

Austerity in the UK has led to the expansion of different kinds of problem debt from those that have historically impacted people (Gardner, Gray and Moser 2020). The proportion of people reporting debt problems relating to government and essential service providers (e.g. electricity, gas, water) – what are often called priority debts – doubled from 21 per cent to 40 per cent in the five years prior to 2019 (Citizens Advice 2018). In 2019, Citizens Advice helped almost 100,000 people who were struggling to make council tax payments – making this the most common debt problem the bureau dealt with that year (Citizens Advice 2019). Research conducted by the debt charity StepChange (2020a) in June 2020 – at the height of the first Covid-19 lockdown in the UK – suggests 2.8 million people were in arrears for utilities, council tax and rent. Another national poll commissioned and published by StepChange (2020b, 2) showed that over half (54 per cent) of those in problem debt receive support through the social security system. However, 43 per cent of those people receiving social security support had used credit to pay for essentials in the last year. The introduction of Universal Credit (UC), with a mandated five-week wait for the first payment, led 92 per cent of respondents to experience some form of hardship or financial difficulty. In summary, state support systems expected to alleviate the problems of poverty are now contributing to and accentuating them instead (Gardner, Gray and Moser 2020).

Around nine million people in the UK could be classified as over-indebted, meaning they 'find keeping up with payments a heavy burden or have fallen behind on, or missed, payments in any three or more months in the last six months', according to a Money and Pensions Service (2019, 5) estimate in 2019. In the same year, national savings were lower in the UK than in any other OECD (Organisation for Economic Co-operation and Development) member country (Barrett 2019), and 22 per cent of UK adults had less than £100 in savings, making them highly vulnerable to a financial shock such as losing their job or incurring unexpected bills (Chapman 2019). During the first year of the Covid-19 pandemic, the unprecedented level of public-policy support, in particular the Coronavirus Job Retention Scheme (i.e. the 'furlough scheme') and the temporary deferral of mortgage payments, mitigated the potential macro-economic impact of the pandemic and enabled more affluent households to pay off debts (Bank of England 2021). However, the picture for the six million households claiming UC by December 2020 was very different. One-third of new UC family claims had no savings before the crisis began, and more than one-fifth of families claiming UC fell behind on essential bills during the crisis, becoming indebted (Brewer and Handscomb 2021). Families claiming UC were more than twice as likely to see increasing levels of debt as a result of Covid-19. For those in debt trouble, there is also a massive shortage of advice services: overall unmet demand was estimated at nearly two million people in the year *before* the Covid-19 pandemic (Money and Pensions Service 2019, 5).

There has also been a shift in who is affected by high levels of debt. In 2019, StepChange reported that not only did record numbers of people contact them in 2018, but over half of those people were in full-time (35 per cent) or part-time (20 per cent) employment (StepChange 2019). This is another indicator of how record levels of employment in the UK prior to Covid-19 hid the fact that the quality of work and levels of remuneration have declined to the point where many jobs simply do not pay for the costs of living. Once again, it is important to note that the burdens of problem debt are not distributed evenly. For instance, 23 per cent of StepChange clients were single parents in 2019, well above the national average of 6 per cent of the adult population. Most of these single parents – 85 per cent – were women. Covid-19 has likely exacerbated these problems, with recent data revealing that over half of all single parents are now in receipt of UC (Brewer and Handscomb 2021, 1). StepChange also reported that the proportion of young people (i.e. those under 40) using their service has risen since the onset of austerity, reaching 65 per cent of service users by 2018.

The situation in the UK is part of a much larger and more troubling global trend. The most recent figures at the time of writing suggest total global debt – that is, money owed by governments, companies and individuals – is 360 per cent of global gross domestic product (GDP) (Strohecker 2021; c.f. Jubilee Debt Campaign 2020). Efforts to pay off this debt have fed directly into in-work poverty, homelessness, rising instances of mental illness and generalised financial precarity. The creation of credit is often underpinned by processes that are extremely harmful to the environment. Debt demands the generation of profit to pay back the original capital plus interest, and thus the constant growth inherent to capitalism. This growth is achieved through the exploitation of human and natural resources and capital-centric ways of thinking about humans and nature as resources to be exploited, which have led to ecological collapse and climate breakdown (Hickel 2020). Such exploitation is also connected to societies becoming more unequal. As fewer people and corporations own key types of scarce assets – such as land, intellectual property, natural resources and digital platforms – everyone else has to pay 'rent' to use these assets or pay interest payments to gain a share (Christophers 2020). This vicious cycle concentrates wealth in fewer hands, enabling further monopolisation of these assets and economic systems in which fewer people have a meaningful voice.

In the Global South, numerous schemes that attempt to alleviate poverty and provoke development have instead created new kinds of vulnerability and harm. Although micro-finance programmes, particularly commercial ones, now increasingly lack credibility in the wake of massive increases in suicides among debtors (Ashta, Khan and Otto 2015), more recent innovations in fintech that have taken place under the banner of financial inclusion seem set to repeat the mistakes of the past (Gabor and Brooks 2017). For instance, recently published research argues that mobile money systems in Kenya like M-Pesa and M-Shwari have created a new form of servitude which accumulates novel kinds of data and commoditises people's behaviours and reputations (Donovan and Park 2019).

Methods for working towards solutions

Clearly, responses that counter the proliferation and intensification of debt are desperately needed as part of broader efforts to envision and engender more inclusive and sustainable forms of prosperity that recognise planetary limits. Key to such efforts will be the multiple forms of expertise that exist both within and beyond the university, and the ways in which these are drawn together. The contributions to this volume embody the belief that collaborative thinking and practice is a necessity if we want to address challenges relating to debt and reimagine the role of finance in shaping, sustaining and securing communities around the world. Collective conversations and partnerships are crucial for channelling diverse sources of inspiration, generating new ideas and linking incipient efforts and experiments so that they might proliferate and grow in scale. Local solutions are as valuable as 'big' ideas because of the different ways in which debt problems are distributed.

The Financing Prosperity Framework (FPN) has been exploring how to reimagine finance since its inception in 2016. As one of the knowledge networks curated by the UCL Institute for Global Prosperity, the FPN brings together people working in the academy, government, business, third-sector organisations and community groups to outline some of the innovations and imaginative solutions already helping – or set to help – people and organisations to address problems of debt. This book represents the culmination of a series of events at which members of the network have explored experiments in better living that address existing debt problems, while creating new forms of flourishing beyond debt. Underpinning these conversations is a curiosity about which insights can potentially be translated to other contexts and/or scaled up and expanded, so that the majority of people in societies around the world can create meaningful lives that are supported, rather than undermined, by financial systems and relations. This book foregrounds some of the innovations and imaginative solutions that members of the FPN are exploring, proposing and/or already implementing. These have been organised into three sections – rethinking debt obligations, rewriting the rules and reworking community economies – to emphasise common themes across the different chapters. However, it is important to note that all authors share an interest in all of these practices.

Rethinking debt obligations

The first section unpacks the moral and social basis of present debt-fuelled economies, challenging the validity of many contemporary forms and modes of debt. Based on work with collaborators at Research for Action, a workers' co-operative producing research to support social, economic and environmental justice, Fanny Malinen discusses the use of citizen debt audits as a tool to scrutinise and challenge the moral and social power of debt. Malinen draws insights from Research for Action's campaign against the use of LOBO (lender option, borrower option) loans by local authorities in the UK. These types of debt subject local authorities to a discipline that forces them to prioritise the interests of financial markets over those of residents. A citizen debt audit in Newham, one of the most indebted and impoverished local authorities in the UK, challenged the legitimacy of Newham's LOBO loan debt and thus its repayment. The audit prompted arguments for the reversal of local government funding cuts and profound changes to regulation of local government finance. The impact of this process has also been scaled up, enabling other councils across the UK to exit LOBO loan contracts early due to public pressure and legal action. Malinen argues that citizen debt audits are a form of collective debt refusal that reveal how financialisation disciplines public authorities to act against the interests of the people they are supposed to serve. They raise questions about lack of oversight and regulation as well as the inability of residents to define what is in the public interest. Ultimately, this prompts a moral reimagining of how local government finances work.

In chapter 3, Nathan Mladin, a researcher working for Theos think tank, uses Christian theology to argue that debt is an issue that is never merely economic: it is also deeply moral and ineradicably social. The chapter develops this insight by using Christian social and political thought to understand debt within the nexus of relationships it articulates, reinforces or adversely affects. While acknowledging that no free-floating 'Christian view on debt' exists, Mladin notes and expounds a set of core ethical concerns and priorities regarding debt relations that run through Christian thought traditions. Building on these, Mladin shows how

Christian social teaching can help reframe and reform contemporary debt so that it honours human dignity, fosters relationships of mutual assistance and inclines towards the common good. He draws in particular on the jubilee tradition of debt cancellation. The chapter offers a series of recommendations for addressing problematic debt, focusing specifically on contemporary applications of the jubilee moral principles of debt forgiveness and cancellation.

Chapter 4, based on an interview conducted by the editors with Martin Groombridge, chief executive officer of London Capital Credit Union (LCCU), explores the ways in which credit unions challenge the moral basis of dominant types of debt relations, which are centred on profit-maximisation motives, by building and promoting explicitly communal forms of credit provision. Credit unions have long offered communities a different kind of debt relation by pooling savings and working towards the mutual benefit of all members. Working in London, one of the so-called 'hearts' of global finance, LCCU is able to utilise the savings of people earning across the income spectrum to provide financial support to those most in need at times of crisis without charging high interest rates to offset the risk of such support. The credit union model helps all members manage their individual financial lives while strengthening communities by curating value locally. A recent innovation in this area is CreditU (2020), a digital platform created by Lindsey Appleyard and her colleagues, which directs users to local credit unions and provides accessible financial information. Regional banking offers another emerging values-led alternative. The Royal Society for Arts (2020) and the Community Savings Bank Association are leading a movement to create 18 regionally focused, mission-led UK community banks.

Rewriting the rules

This section of the book foregrounds legal and political methods for changing the rules of the system to provide debt relief to those who most need it and reshape national and household economies for more inclusive and sustainable prosperity. The section starts with Joe Spooner's chapter on bankruptcy. Spooner, a legal studies scholar at the London School of Economics and Political Science (LSE), argues that bankruptcy law can play an expanded role in addressing the UK's debt crisis by operating as a social insurer of last resort, providing a safety net for desperate households and acting as an 'automatic stabilizer' to rebalance the wider economy. Noting the geographical differences in legal systems, Spooner argues that debtors can be offered a 'fresh start' through the basic principle of bankruptcy law – that a person who is unable to pay their debts should receive a 'discharge' or cancellation of those debts at the end of a bankruptcy process (which in England and Wales lasts for one year), on complying with certain conditions (including making available to creditors any assets and income beyond those required for a reasonable standard of living). The bankruptcy process frees up resources for use in funding household living costs, which are then returned to the Real Economy via household expenditure. The economic losses of bankruptcy are redistributed away from households and towards the financial sector, both reducing inequality and leaving more money in the pockets of those with the 'highest marginal propensity to consume' – i.e. low- and middle-income households who will spend proportionally more of their disposable income. Spooner's argument is that expanded access to and use of bankruptcy procedures can enable the consumption needed for economic growth, while offering significant health, psychological and emotional benefits for those struggling with debt.

In chapter 6, Johnna Montgomerie draws on the history of debt jubilees (cancellations) and the bailout of the financial sector in 2008 to argue for a household debt write-off. Montgomerie, a political economist at King's College London, proposes the use of a long-term refinancing operation (LTRO) – a well-established monetary tool – to give UK households access to 0 per cent refinancing on up to £25,000 of debt. This write-down option will provide immediate relief to households by reducing their debt-servicing costs and will allow lenders to spread the losses to anticipated future interest revenue over the longer term. It gives households access to government-subsidised low interest rates, which have been enjoyed by financial institutions and large corporations for nearly two decades. The advantage of an LTRO is that borrowers can use it to target specific types of debts (such as payday loans) that cause the most harm to their household's balance sheet, without policymakers having to determine which households are worthy of debt write-down and which are not: all households have access to refinancing. This proposal re-engineers the current credit-based monetary system to create something new: an economy where the risks, rewards, wealth and harms are evenly shared between lenders and borrowers. This requires a reconfiguration of the governance of credit – by finance ministries, central banks and regulators – so that it operates as an economic utility for the benefit of the public. Debt will no longer be the purveyor of perpetual financial crisis that leads to the destruction of people's economic security and well-being. Instead it will serve a useful purpose as a form of sustainable and long-term investment in a better collective future.

In chapter 7, Josh Ryan-Collins, an economist at UCL, seeks to rewrite the rules of an economic system that has made house prices unaffordable for many. He argues that the demand for landed property has become excessive and speculative. Banking systems have become primarily real estate lenders, creating credit and money that flows into an existing and fixed supply of land. This pushes up house prices, creating ever more demand for mortgage credit and higher profits for banks. To address this problem, Ryan-Collins argues that a number of coordinated responses are required. Housing needs to be thought about primarily as a source of shelter, not a financial asset. Deep systemic reforms are required, which maintain tight control over mortgage credit creation. Subsidies that governments have showered on homeownership should be employed to stimulate capital investment and innovation in more productive sectors of the economy. The public sector must also take a much more interventionist role in shaping the land market, ensuring it creates public value, not just short-term capital gains or rentier incomes for speculative domestic and international investors. Retaining public control over land and the usage of land is key. This will enable public and co-operative housing systems to be properly funded. Taxation systems in general need to move away from labour and towards land rents. Such measures should be complemented by the creation or expansion of state investment banks and stakeholder banks that provide long-term, high-risk capital to support innovation and provide the next generation of infrastructure needed to support the transition to a low-carbon economy.

It is also worth briefly noting a number of other ways in which members of the FPN are seeking to rewrite the rules of the current economic system. The Institute for Global Prosperity's (2017) proposal for Universal Basic Services seeks to massively expand and transform the provision of public services to eliminate the need for debt in many circumstances. In South Africa, academic research by James (2015) and campaigning by activist organisation Black Sash (Jordaan 2017) have led to legal challenges to practices through which debt repayments are forcibly reclaimed by creditors through the social grant system. In the UK, the End the Debt Trap campaign, led by the New Economics Foundation (2020), demands that interest rates and charges on all forms of consumer credit should be capped. Collectively, this work illustrates that the political and economic rules of the game are always in the process of being contested and rewritten.

Reworking community economies

The final section of the book, reworking community economies, draws together chapters on community-embedded work that is changing the role of debt in economic, social and political life. Efforts to rewrite the rules discussed in the previous section, which often foreground the national scale as the site of intervention, will only succeed if they are aligned with more local-scale action to deal with debts and amplify more ethical forms of credit provision.

In chapter 8, Hilary Powell and Dan Edelstyn, artists and filmmakers who founded the Hoe Street Central Bank (HSCB), explore the role of imagination and local grassroots experiments in reworking the economy so that it functions in a more just manner. HSCB was created as part of 'Bank Job', a participatory artistic project and community action that ultimately resulted in debt cancellation and a feature film that traced the process. In early 2018, the authors moved into the former Co-Op Bank on Hoe Street in Walthamstow, London, and opened HSCB. Together with a team of local people they printed their own banknotes and bonds, held a range of community events and education sessions for residents, schoolchildren and university students. Sale of the banknotes raised over £40,000. Half of this money was donated to local charities at the front lines of combatting the negative effects of austerity. The other half was used to buy over one million pounds of 'bad debt' in the form of local payday loans on secondary markets. This debt was then forgiven, providing concrete assistance to those caught at the sharp end of problematic debt. However, the authors argue that the collective power of art, sharing and community action is more important in terms of the inspiration and challenge it offers. The Bank Job project, which is already being imitated by other communities across the UK, provides hope that communities can be resilient and fight together against an unjust economic system that has socialised losses and privatised gains.

Chapter 9, a collaboration between Christopher Harker, an interdisciplinary scholar working at the UCL Institute for Global Prosperity, and Jerry During, co-founder and executive director of Money Advice and Education (Money A+E), focuses on the problem of isolation that many debtors face and how this can be challenged through community-based organisations. Using the work of Money A+E, a London-wide debt advice service, the chapter argues for innovations in the advice sector that focus on communities rather than individuals and the use of broader social networks to support those struggling with debt. Money A+E does this by getting community members to become mentors to their peers, while supporting campaigns for broader solutions that combat poverty by addressing high housing costs and low-paying work and cancelling debt. The lived experiences of debt that form the basis of Money A+E's interventions draw attention to the social inequalities that striate British society. Many current debt problems are experienced unequally not just according to class, but also according to race. Money A+E's work specifically targets historically disadvantaged economic communities. The chapter argues that Money A+E's work actively contributes to building and sustaining forms of prosperity that are particularly salient to the marginalised communities within which they work.

In chapter 10, Charlotte Johnson, an interdisciplinary scholar working at UCL's Institute for Sustainable Resources, examines the connections between domestic infrastructures and debt. The technical systems – water, energy, waste – that turn housing into a habitable space which is warm, ventilated and light have increasingly been entangled with financial infrastructures. In some cases this has led to problems including evictions and electricity being cut off when people cannot afford rising costs. These entanglements of technology and finance, and the new forms of precarity, inequality and indebtedness they are creating, are crucial because they underpin and support low-carbon transitions. This is particularly evident in housing (re)developments with new but expensive low-carbon infrastructure like heat networks. Johnson argues that community-led transition initiatives offer alternative mechanisms to finance new local energy systems that deliver low-cost, context-sensitive energy solutions. The case of People Powered Retrofit (PPR) is presented to demonstrate how existing built environments can become assets to generate shared income and social value. These ideas invite further exploration of recent work by other members of the FPN on circular bio-economies that use nature-based solutions to meet everyday needs (Costanza et al. 2020). Such work points out not only that debt is contributing to climate emergency, but also that climate emergency threatens to undermine dominant debt-based economies by introducing unquantifiable risks and undermining the ecological systems that underpin human forms of production and reproduction.

Financing prosperity by dealing with debt

Taken together, the FPN's efforts to rethink debt obligations, rewrite the rules producing widespread and damaging indebtedness and rework community economies provide a series of interlinked proposals and actions through which financial practices and relationships can be reformatted, creating pathways towards more inclusive, just and sustainable prosperity. In conclusion, UCL economic geographer Amy Horton draws out how the diverse contemporary debt relations and multiple routes towards prosperity that are illustrated in the book pose challenging questions for austerity politics and democracy. Horton builds on these themes by opening up a discussion around care economies. As she notes, efforts to meet the urgent global challenge of planetary emergency through different economic systems must also find ways to finance the sustainable interdependence which, in concert with our ecosystems, provides the foundation for all social life. We hope that when readers reach the conclusion, they are not only inspired to participate in and even provoke change but also have examples and imaginative resources that will help them to do so.

Notes

1   In this report, financial debt is distinguished from debt secured against property.

References

Ashta, A., Khan, S., and Otto, P. 2015. 'Does microfinance cause or reduce suicides? Policy recommendations for reducing borrower stress', *Briefings in Entrepreneurial Finance* 24 (2): 165–90.

Bank of England 2021. Household debt and Covid. Quarterly bulletin 2021 Q2. Accessed 29 November 2021. https://www.bankofengland.co.uk/quarterly-bulletin/2021/2021-q2/household-debt-and-covid.

Barrett, C. 2019. 'Inside the UK's debt crisis', *Financial Times*. 26 April 2019. Accessed 1 July 2021. https://www.ft.com/content/1ea8527a-5464-11e9-91f9-b6515a54c5b1.

Blakeley, G. 2019. 'Theresa May's plan to bribe Labour MPs to back Brexit shows austerity was always a choice', *New Statesman*. 31 January 2019. Accessed 1 July 2021. https://www.newstatesman.com/politics/economy/2019/01/theresa-may-s-plan-bribe-labour-mps-back-brexit-shows-austerity-was-always.

Blyth, M. 2013. *Austerity: The history of a dangerous idea*. Oxford: Oxford University Press.

Brewer, M., and Handscomb, K. 2021. 'The debts that divide us: Flash findings from a survey of families claiming Universal Credit'. 7 February 2021. London: Resolution Foundation. Accessed 1 July 2021. https://www.resolutionfoundation.org/app/uploads/2021/02/The-debts-that-divide-us.pdf.

Chamon, M., and Ostry, J. 2021. 'A future with high public debt: Low-for-long is not low forever', *IMFBlog*. 20 April 2021. Accessed 1 July 2021. https://blogs.imf.org/2021/04/20/a-future-with-high-public-debt-low-for-long-is-not-low-forever/.

Chapman, B. 2019. 'Britain owes £72.5bn on credit cards as households pile on debt despite fears for economy', *The Independent*. 4 January 2019. Accessed 1 July 2021. https://www.independent.co.uk/news/business/news/credit-card-debt-household-bank-of-england-consumer-november-uk-economy-a8712271.html.

Christophers, B. 2020. *Rentier Capitalism: Who owns the economy, and who pays for it?* London: Verso Books.

Citizens Advice. 2018. 'Hidden debts: The growing problem of being behind on bills and in debt to the government'. Accessed 7 February 2022. https://www.citizensadvice.org.uk/about-us/our-work/policy/policy-research-topics/debt-and-money-policy-research/hidden-debts-the-growing-problem-of-being-behind-on-bills-and-in-debt-to-the-government/.

Citizens Advice. 2019. 'The costs of collection: The high price of council tax debt collection'. Accessed 1 July 2021. https://www.citizensadvice.org.uk/about-us/our-work/policy/policy-research-topics/debt-and-money-policy-research/the-costs-of-collection-the-high-price-of-council-tax-debt-collection/.

Costanza, R., Kubiszewski, I., Lovins, H., Giovannini, E., Fioramonti, L., Dixson-Declève, S., McGlade, J., Pickett, K., Wilkinson, R., Wallis, S., Trebeck, K., and Ragnarsdóttir, K. V. 2020. 'Investing in nature to transform the post COVID-19 economy. A 10-point action plan to create a circular bioeconomy devoted to sustainable wellbeing', *Solutions*. 14 May 2020. Accessed 1 July 2021. https://thesolutionsjournal.com/2020/05/14/investing-in-nature-to-transform-the-post-covid-19-economy-a-10-point-action-plan-to-create-a-circular-bioeconomy-devoted-to-sustainable-wellbeing/.

CreditU. 2020. 'How can Credit U help you?' https://www.creditu.co.uk/about-us. Accessed 7 February 2022.

Donovan, K., and Park, E. 2019. 'Perpetual debt in the Silicon Savannah', *Boston Review*. 20 September 2019. Accessed 1 July 2021. http://bostonreview.net/class-inequality-global-justice/kevin-p-donovan-emma-park-perpetual-debt-silicon-savannah.

Financial Conduct Authority. 2019. 'Commentary on Mortgage lending statistics – December 2019', 10 December 2019. Accessed 7 February 2022. https://www.fca.org.uk/data/mortgage-lending-statistics/commentary-mortgage-lending-statistics-december-2019.

Gabor, D., and Brooks, S. 2017. 'The digital revolution in financial inclusion: International development in the fintech era', *New Political Economy* 22(4): 423–36.

Gardner, J., Gray, M., and Moser, K. 2020. *Debt and Austerity*. Cheltenham, UK: Edward Elgar Publishing.

Gibson-Graham, J. K., Cameron, J., and Healy, S. 2013. *Take Back the Economy: An ethical guide for transforming our communities*. Minneapolis: University of Minnesota Press.

Giles, C. 2020. 'IMF says austerity is not inevitable to ease pandemic impact on public finances', *Financial Times*. 14 October 2020. Accessed 1 July 2021. https://www.ft.com/content/722ef9c0-36f6-4119-a00b-06d33fced78f.

Graeber, D. 2011. *Debt: The first 5,000 years*. London: Melville House Publishing.

Han, X., Medas, P., and Yang, S. 2021. 'The pre-pandemic debt landscape – and why it matters', *IMFBlog*. 1 February 2021. Accessed 1 July 2021. https://blogs.imf.org/2021/02/01/the-pre-pandemic-debt-landscape-and-why-it-matters/.

Harker, C., Huq, Z., and Charalambous, E. 2020. Covid-19 as a Challenge to Prosperity: The case of Money A+E service users. London: UCL Institute for Global Prosperity. Accessed 1 July 2021. https://www.ucl.ac.uk/bartlett/igp/sites/bartlett/files/covid_19_as_a_challenge_to_prosperity.pdf.

Hickel, J. 2020. *Less is More: How degrowth will save the world*. London: Penguin Random House.

Inman, P., and Barr, C. 2017. 'The UK's debt crisis – In figures', *Guardian*. 18 September 2017. Accessed 1 July 2021. https://www.theguardian.com/business/2017/sep/18/uk-debt-crisis-credit-cards-car-loans.

Inman, P., and Wearden, G. 2020. 'Covid-19 drives UK national debt to £2tn for first time', *Guardian*. 22 August 2020. Accessed 1 July 2021. https://www.theguardian.com/business/2020/aug/21/covid-19-drives-uk-national-debt-to-2tn-for-first-time.

Institute for Global Prosperity. 2017. *Social Prosperity for the Future: A proposal for Universal Basic Services*. London: UCL Institute for Global Prosperity. Accessed 1 July 2021. https://www.ucl.ac.uk/bartlett/igp/sites/bartlett/files/universal_basic_services_-_the_institute_for_global_prosperity_.pdf.

James, D. 2015. *Money from Nothing: Indebtedness and aspiration in South Africa*. Stanford, CA: Stanford University Press.

Jordaan, N. 2017. 'Garnishee ruling a "setback for poor"', *TimesLIVE*. 10 May 2017. Accessed 1 July 2021. https://www.timeslive.co.za/news/south-africa/2017-05-10-garnishee-ruling-a-setback-for-poor/.

Jubilee Debt Campaign. 2019. 'Personal debt grows six times more than wages', 1 March 2019. Accessed 1 July 2021. https://jubileedebt.org.uk/press-release/personal-debt-grows-six-times-more-than-wages.

Jubilee Debt Campaign. 2020. 'How big is global debt?', Accessed 1 July 2021. https://jubileedebt.
org.uk/#0.

Langley, P. 2014. *Liquidity Lost: The Governance of the Global Financial Crisis.* Oxford: Oxford
University Press.

Lazzarato, M. 2012. *The Making of Indebted Man.* Los Angeles, CA: Semiotext(e).

Lazzarato, M. 2015. *Governing by Debt.* Los Angeles, CA: Semiotext(e).

Money and Pensions Service, 2019. *Mapping the Unmet Demand for Debt Advice in the UK.* Money
and Pensions Service. Accessed 7 February 2022. https://www.moneyadviceplus.org.uk/
wp-content/uploads/2019/06/supply-2018-participant-report.pdf.

Moore, H. 2015. 'Global prosperity and sustainable development goals', *Journal of International
Development* 27(6): 801–15.

Moore, H., and Mintchev, N. 2021. *What is Prosperity?* London: UCL Institute for Global
Prosperity. Accessed 1 July 2021. https://discovery.ucl.ac.uk/id/eprint/10126424/7/
Moore_WP_What%20is%20Prosperity_DOI.pdf.

Narayan, K. 2020. *Household Debt and Problem Debt in British Cities.* London: Centre for Cities.
Accessed 1 July 2021. https://www.centreforcities.org/wp-content/uploads/2020/04/
Household-debt-and-problem-debt-in-British-cities-1.pdf.

New Economics Foundation. 2020. 'End the debt trap', Accessed 1 July 2021. https://
neweconomics.org/campaigns/end-the-debt-trap.

Office for National Statistics (ONS). 2019. *Dataset: Household debt: Wealth in Great Britain.*
Newport: Office for National Statistics. Accessed 1 July 2021. https://www.ons.gov.uk/
peoplepopulationandcommunity/personalandhouseholdfinances/incomeandwealth/
datasets/householddebtwealthingreatbritain.

Raworth, K. 2017. *Doughnut Economics.* London: Chelsea Green Publishing.

Research for Action. 2018. *Debt and Democracy in Newham: A citizen audit of LOBO loans.* London:
Research for Action. Accessed 1 July 2021. https://researchforaction.uk/?ddownload=537.

Royal Society for Arts. 2020. 'Regional banking', Accessed 1 July 2021. https://www.thersa.org/
discover/topics/regional-banking.

StepChange. 2019. *Personal Debt in the UK. 2018 Statistics Yearbook.* Leeds: StepChange.
Accessed 1 July 2021. https://www.stepchange.org/Portals/0/documents/Reports/2018-
statistics-yearbook-stepchange-debt-charity.pdf.

StepChange. 2020a. 'Coronavirus and personal debt: A financial recovery strategy for
households', June 2020. Accessed 1 July 2021. https://www.stepchange.org/Portals/0/
assets/pdf/coronavirus-policy-briefing-stepchange.pdf.

StepChange. 2020b. 'Problem debt and the social security system', January 2020. Accessed 1 July
2021. https://www.stepchange.org/Portals/0/assets/pdf/social-security-mini-brief-report.pdf.

Strohecker, K. 2021. 'IIF: Global debt levels decline for the first time in 2-1/2 years', *Reuters.* 13 May
2021. Accessed 1 July 2021. https://www.reuters.com/article/global-debt-iif-idUSL1N2N00ZU.

Trades Union Congress. 2020. 'Unsecured debt hits new peak of £14,540 per household – TUC
analysis', 10 January 2020. Accessed 1 July 2021. https://www.tuc.org.uk/news/
unsecured-debt-hits-new-peak-ps14540-household-tuc-analysis.

Part 1
Rethinking debt obligations

2
Building democracy through challenging financialisation: a citizen debt audit of local government bank loans

Fanny Malinen, Research for Action

A citizen debt audit is a tool for scrutinising and thereby starting to unravel the power of debt. Like so many different debts, local government debt subjects councils to a discipline that forces them to prioritise the interests of financial markets over those of residents. This has been made especially visible by austerity. As part of the workers' co-operative Research for Action and, prior to this, the activist group Debt Resistance UK, I have participated in a citizen audit of local authority debt in the UK, in which we focused on a type of bank loan called LOBO (lender option, borrower option). This chapter is based on a report Research for Action published in 2018 called *Debt and Democracy in Newham: A citizen audit of LOBO debt* (Research for Action 2018a), which focused on the East London borough of Newham, the most indebted council in the country and one of the most impoverished, detailing why Newham's LOBO loan debt is illegitimate and should not be paid. We also recommended the reversal of funding cuts and profound changes to oversight and regulation of local government finance.

The audit has been a powerful act, as is shown by councils exiting LOBO loan contracts early and taking legal action (Makortoff 2019a). However, LOBO loans are not only an example of illegitimate debt; they are also symptomatic of how financialisation leads public authorities to act against the interests of the people they are supposed to serve, and how the superiority of finance has become so embedded in our society that it goes unquestioned. The LOBO loan scandal does not end with the renegotiation of the loans. That most UK councils have been sold risky and complex financial products has exposed the inadequacy of the guidance, regulation and oversight in local government finance. The inability of residents to have their objections heard when their councils are being financialised shows the need for reimagining the public's role in scrutinising public spending and demanding accountability.

Illegitimate debt

At the heart of a debt audit is defining what debt is illegitimate and should not be repaid. As part of Research for Action's work, we have analysed LOBO loan debt according to the contracting, origin and servicing of the debt. Our work has been influenced by the Platform for Citizen Debt Audit (PACD) in the Spanish state,[1] which defines a citizen debt audit as 'a process to, collectively, understand how we have arrived at the current situation; what economic, social, cultural, environmental, gender and political impacts has this indebtedness created' (PACD 2013).

There are various ways to conduct a debt audit, depending on who leads the process. This could be the indebted government; social movements or concerned citizens; the lender itself; an independent external body; or combinations of these. However, official entities will rarely take strong action without at least some pressure from the civil society.

Calls for debt audits have a long history that goes back to the 1980s debt crisis that ravaged the Global South. Ecuador was the first country to realise an official audit in 2008, led by the government of President Rafael Correa following pressure from social movements. The debt audit commission consisted of independent international experts and examined the country's loans from international financial institutions. They found that much of it resulted from corruption and lack of transparency and did not benefit the people of Ecuador. Following the findings of the audit, the country defaulted on $3.2 billion. Ecuador later strategically bought back much of the debt for a third of the original value, freeing up funds to be used for social spending instead of debt repayments.

Following the financial crisis and the bailouts that brought the debt crisis to the Global North, social movements in Europe started demanding the non-payment of loans they deemed illegitimate. This was the case especially in Greece and the Spanish state, which were both hit hardest by the eurozone crisis. In 2015, as part of the first Syriza government, the Speaker of the Greek Parliament, Zoe Konstantopoulou, initiated an official debt audit committee after years of pressure from social movements, especially ELE, the Greek Debt Audit Campaign, which was part of the strong mobilisations against European Union (EU)-imposed austerity measures. This 'Debt Truth Committee' produced an interim report that declared a lot of the country's debt – which resulted from the bailouts of the Troika (the EU, International Monetary Fund and European Central Bank) – illegal, illegitimate and odious. However, the committee's work was cut short by the government capitulating to creditor demands, signing a new bailout deal with the EU and calling snap elections.

Similarly, the financial crisis sparked citizens across the Spanish state to organise local debt audits as part of the PACD. They worked collectively to expose the illegitimacy of loans that did not serve the public interest. Loans were often taken out in the pre-crash lending boom and used for infrastructure projects that quickly proved to be 'white elephants': expensive but without the value to justify the cost. Following the Spanish 2015 municipal elections that lifted progressive municipalist platforms into power, many councils undertook debt audits. A 2012 change in the Spanish constitution forced local authorities to prioritise debt payments over social spending. Many councils have disobeyed this law, and in 2016, hundreds of elected politicians made their opposition public in a manifesto. Madrid, the capital, initiated an official audit of debt and public policy that analysed the council's economic policies through a lens of economic and gender inequality as well as environmental sustainability. The plan was to have a participatory phase that would engage neighbourhood assemblies in the discussion of illegitimacy, although the official aim of the audit was not the non-payment of the debt. However, the audit was jeopardised when the council member for Economy and Finance Carlos Sánchez Mato, who was driving the institutional part of the process, was removed in late 2017. In the May 2019 elections, the Right returned to power in Madrid, and the audit report never saw daylight. Similarly, in many other councils the municipalist progressive Left's moment in power did not last.

Rejecting the payment of odious, illegal or illegitimate debt to enable the prioritisation of human rights – such as the right to health care and education – over debt repayments is the unifying aim of all debt audit movements. However, citizen debt audit movements have a broader focus than the technical process of examining contracts to detect these specific types of loans. Part of the transformative nature of citizen debt audits is that they do not only treat the debt as a source of economic inequality: they also examine the oppressive dimensions of it. As austerity measures affect women, communities of colour, disabled people and sexual and gender minorities disproportionately, citizen debt audit movements also have these issues at their heart. As Jezabel Goudinoff from PACD Barcelona explained in 2015 (Malinen 2015),

> We think illegitimacy is a political concept and what is illegitimate or legitimate needs to be decided by the people, society as a whole. This is why we need a citizens' audit that goes beyond the financial ... We understand it as a tool of social transformation and, as such, permanent.

Illegal debt

Where illegitimacy of debt is a political concept and decided through a societal conversation, there are also plenty of examples of illegal lending, determined by the judicial system. Court cases that have led to debt cancellation have usually been brought about by political pressure. As a result of our work on LOBO loans, seven local authorities in the UK took joint legal action against Barclays, one of the banks that had sold them LOBOs. Newham Council took its own action against Barclays as well as the Royal Bank of Scotland (RBS), which resulted in the council successfully renegotiating its LOBO loans with NatWest, a subsidiary of RBS, before the case entered court (Makortoff 2019b). In February 2021, a judge ruled in favour of Barclays on the cases brought by Newham and the other councils. After an appeal by Newham Council, the case was settled in February 2022.

There is a precedent of local authority debt cancellation in the UK from the 1980s. Throughout that decade, 137 UK councils had been encouraged by banks and brokers to enter into multiple interest-rate-swap agreements. Hammersmith and Fulham Council in West London had signed hundreds of swap contracts with investment bank Goldman Sachs, risking potential losses of £300 million of taxpayers' money. When interest rates moved in favour of the banks, the council's default became a realistic possibility. The High Court ruled in 1989 that entering into standalone swaps and derivative contracts was *ultra vires*, or outside the councils' legal powers. Despite an appeal by the banks, in 1991 the House of Lords upheld the ruling, deciding that it was not the council's role to be speculating upon interest rates and taxpayers should not be held liable. The contracts were cancelled. More recently, Italian municipalities including Milan were mis-sold derivatives by London-based banks. The banks settled with Milan in 2012, paying the city almost 500 million euros and terminating the contracts. In November 2011, the High Court of Paris dismissed the Royal Bank of Scotland's request for Saint-Étienne in central France to pay swaps the bank claimed it was owed. The judge recognised the elected officials' argument that the speculative product had been wrongly proposed to the cities and that there was a lack of information on the part of the banks on the risks of such complex products. In the United States, a group of cities led by Baltimore and the Central Bucks School District in Pennsylvania accused banks of conspiring to fix prices for municipal derivatives, causing them to receive lower interest rates than they would have received in a competitive marketplace. The resulting legal action prompted settlements against the banks amounting to hundreds of millions of pounds.

Methodology of the citizen audit

At the heart of the citizen debt audit of LOBO loans has been a quest for information. The project started with the work of two now-defunct organisations, Move Your Money and Debt Resistance UK, which made extensive use of the Freedom of Information Act to uncover the extent of councils' LOBO borrowing across the country. Based on this, Debt Resistance UK was able to compile a public database of LOBO loans and provide information to journalists. We also used campaigning tools like submissions to inquiries, open letters and shareholder activism.

There has been a large amount of media coverage on LOBO loans generated by the campaign. One of the most impactful reports was the documentary 'How councils blow your millions' for Channel 4's *Dispatches* in 2015, as it sparked a parliamentary inquiry into local government bank loans – which was then discontinued without reason or conclusion. However, it provided a lot of analysis by financial experts and brought this into the public realm.

As a result of councils initiating legal action against banks in 2018 and 2019, there has been increasing interest from councillors and residents who want to find out more about their councils' LOBO loans and take action. We worked with residents throughout the audit: perhaps the most important dimension of a citizen debt audit is a connection with residents and those adversely affected by the payment of illegitimate debt.

In the Newham audit, residents played a key role in providing us with information about the consequences of continuing the payment of illegitimate debt. In many cases, this took the form of an exchange of information, where we shared our research on LOBO loans and the council's financial situation. This exchange enabled us to strengthen our arguments about the illegitimacy of the loans and provided anti-austerity and housing campaigners with tools to argue against the council's line that there was no money to provide essential services.

We also had important allies in councillors who wanted to see LOBO borrowing scrutinised in their boroughs. They often found it difficult to get information on LOBO loans and were attacked politically for suggesting that the council's financial decisions needed scrutiny. Newham is a one-party council, and its Audit Board was at the time chaired by the cabinet member for finance, which raises important questions about the checks and balances on local democracy and accountability. The leadership of Newham Council has since changed.

One of the key ways in which residents have participated in auditing their councils' LOBO loans is by filing objections to their councils' accounts. Under the 2014 Local Audit and Accountability Act, residents can object to spending that they do not believe to be in the public interest or that could be unlawful. Debt Resistance UK and Research for Action supported over 50 residents to use this right. The objections were useful in spreading awareness of the issue, for example creating media coverage and reaching out to local groups. However, they did not serve their purpose: to make the councils' auditors examine whether the loans were in the public interest or refer them to court. In a report published in 2021, *Democracy Denied: Audit and accountability failure in local government* (Research for Action 2021),[2] we detailed the shortcomings of the objection process. Of the 83 cases followed in that report – which concerned private finance initiative (PFI) projects in addition to LOBO loans – not a single one resulted in action by the auditors. Worse still, some did not even receive a reply, and where auditors investigated the issues, they took on average two years to provide responses that showed a limited understanding of local government finance and little engagement with the arguments residents had raised.

Residents were often restricted from sharing the auditors' correspondence, at least until the auditor reached a final view, and felt dismissed, intimidated and sidelined by the process. Sharing restrictions meant they were not able to involve their communities in discussing what was a collective issue: the use of public funds. Citizen audits have at their heart a much deeper notion of accountability than simply a demand for transparency. Access to information is not enough if we do not have ownership over it and cannot use it for educational purposes. In other words, the challenge for a citizen audit is to bring that about in a world where conversations about finance, or even the economy, are not dominated by those in power – and where the position of being a financial expert is itself not a form of power.

Local government austerity

Core funding from central government to local government was cut by 49.1 per cent between the financial years of 2010/11 and 2017/18 as part of a total overhaul of how local government is financed (National Audit Office [NAO] 2018). Reducing funding to local authorities has been a key part of the fiscal austerity economic agenda since its outset in 2010, as local government spending amounts to approximately a quarter of UK public spending. The reforms were phased in, which is why the near collapse of council services happened gradually and quietly – at least until the Covid-19 pandemic hit. In 2020, central government supported local government with an estimated £9.1 billion, which helped to keep local authorities afloat in the crisis (NAO 2021). However, this has not given the sector certainty over long-term funding or an ability to plan. Rather, the state and future of local government funding are further obscured by short-term emergency measures.

In real terms, the cuts between 2010 and 2018 amounted to a 28.6 per cent reduction in spending power, as the funding cuts have to some extent been offset by increases in council tax and business rates. Most councils are increasing council tax and charging for services to make ends meet; this has had an impact, particularly on those on low incomes. Local authorities also receive grants to fund statutory services like education and social care.

Funding cuts have been felt unevenly: according to the NAO, in the most deprived fifth of areas, funding per resident has been cut by 36 per cent, compared to 22 per cent in the least deprived areas. Alongside these cuts, local authorities have had to respond to a growing demand for key statutory services, particularly in response to crises in adult and children's social care and homelessness. This has been the case since before the pandemic: from 2010/11 to 2016/17, the number of households assessed as homeless and entitled to temporary accommodation in England increased by 33.9 per cent; the number of looked-after children grew by

10.9 per cent; and the estimated number of people in need of care aged 65 and over increased by 14.3 per cent (NAO 2018).

A combination of reduced funding and higher demand has meant that a growing number of local authorities have not managed to remain within their budgets and have relied on reserves to balance their books. The NAO estimated in 2018 that 10.6 per cent of local authorities with social care responsibilities have the equivalent of less than three years' worth of reserves left if they continue to use them at the rate they did in 2016/17. Relying on reserves and short-term funding initiatives put in place by central government to address the social care funding crisis are not a sustainable alternative to a long-term funding plan.

There is significant uncertainty as to how local government will be financed in the 2020s. In February 2018, Northamptonshire County Council issued a notice saying it was unable to balance its books, the equivalent of going bankrupt. In late 2020, Croydon Council followed suit. A 2018 survey among council officials suggested that 80 per cent of councils fear for their financial sustainability and that they could follow suit. The pandemic has only added to this uncertainty, reducing local authorities' income streams from services such as leisure centres and parking and creating more work related to the health emergency.

The Public Accounts Committee has raised concerns regarding the effectiveness of the scrutiny of local government by the Ministry for Housing, Communities and Local Government (now called the Department for Levelling Up, Housing and Communities). In the 2018 *Financial Sustainability of Local Authorities* inquiry, the Committee wrote: 'The Department does not have a consistent and transparent method to assess financial risk in local authorities . . . There is therefore no shared definition of what financial sustainability means in practice in the local authority sector' (Public Accounts Committee 2018).

This overhaul in the way local government is financed is only one chapter in a story. Austerity is more than just cuts to services. It marks a deliberate shift in power relations whereby, with declining public spending, public scrutiny and democratic accountability are also eroded. Decisions are increasingly made as purely administrative actions by unelected officials based on economic rationale, not social necessity. Instead of providers of public services that need guaranteed and stable funding, local authorities are treated as commercial actors encouraged to borrow from capital markets, hedge against risk and engage in speculative activities. Through financialisation, risk is introduced into the funding of essential services.

Debt is central to disciplining councils to play by the rules of financial capital. Interest payments are ring-fenced in councils' budgets, which means savings have to be made elsewhere, as the failure to service debts would lead to hefty financial penalties and the imposition of government administrators. This forces councils to prioritise paying banks above everything else. It also lays bare the power dynamic between the cash-strapped public sector and financial institutions with balance sheets that are multiples of local authorities' collective budgets. Yet rescuing these same financial institutions is what prompted the wave of public-sector cutbacks.

Effects of austerity

The violence of austerity has been well documented. Perhaps the most damning account came in late 2018 when United Nations Special Rapporteur Philip Alston visited the UK to find out about human rights and extreme poverty. The Special Rapporteur's report summary is worth quoting at length:

> And local authorities, especially in England, which perform vital roles in providing a real social safety net have been gutted by a series of government policies. Libraries have closed in record numbers, community and youth centers have been shrunk and underfunded, public spaces and buildings including parks and recreation centers have been sold off. While the labour and housing markets provide the crucial backdrop, the focus of this report is on the contribution made by social security and related policies. The results? Fourteen million people, a fifth of the population, live in poverty. Four million of these are more than 50% below the poverty line, and 1.5 million are destitute, unable to afford basic essentials. The widely respected Institute for Fiscal Studies predicts a 7% rise in child poverty between 2015 and 2022, and various sources predict child poverty rates of as high as 40%. For almost one in every two children to be poor in twenty-first century Britain is not just a disgrace, but a social calamity and an economic disaster, all rolled into one (Alston 2018).

Documenting the extent to which austerity has devastated lives and communities was an important dimension of our debt audit in Newham. We spoke to residents, asking them about their experiences with austerity and council democracy. This took the form of interviews with randomly selected users of council services but also workshops and group interviews with campaigners, community groups and charities working to pick up the slack for those whose lives have been devastated by service cuts and the housing crisis. We published the findings of our 51 interviews with randomly selected residents in a report called *Cuts and Contempt*. Only a third of our respondents felt that their needs are met by the council, and most felt that the council's spending priorities did not reflect their needs. Lack of services, increased barriers to proving eligibility for support, loss of benefits and increased charging for services caused stress, financial difficulties and mental and physical health problems for residents (Research for Action 2018b).

Local government borrowing

Although the harshest austerity has been felt in the last decade, the changes in local government finance have been underway for longer. One of these has been the increase in borrowing since the Local Government Act 2003, which gave local authorities powers to set their own borrowing limits and to borrow from any willing lender without consulting the central government, provided the borrowing was prudential and in British pounds. The Chartered Institute of Public Finance and Accountancy (CIPFA) issues a Prudential Code to guide this borrowing and authorities have to report to central government, but the scrutiny over whether borrowing is within those guidelines sits with the council's external auditor, and there is no central oversight.

Most council borrowing is through the Public Works Loan Board (PWLB), the statutory body through which central government lends to local authorities. The PWLB offers both fixed (up to 50 years) and variable rate (up to 10 years) loans, and its interest rates are determined by the Debt Management Office in a transparent way enshrined in legislation. The PWLB also offers lower interest rates for loans that are to be used for specific purposes, for example infrastructure, and is the lender of last resort to local authorities: should a council be in financial difficulty, the PWLB can intervene. It was announced in 2016 that the PWLB would be abolished, but details of future arrangements have not been announced.

The audit regime has also been re-engineered since 2010. The Local Audit and Accountability Act 2014 introduced private companies into local government audits in England, abolishing the Audit Commission. Throughout our audit, we have attempted to engage with the auditors through public rights set out in the Act. This has only served to highlight the problems that arise from giving private companies the power to define what spending is in the public interest. With the closure of the Audit Commission, an important oversight function was lost too, with oversight currently being fragmented across different bodies, none of which specifically have the responsibility for local audits.

That local authorities are audited by private companies and there is no public oversight over their decisions emphasises the importance of citizen action in scrutinising public spending decisions. However, it is also highly problematic to scale back the functions of the state and expect people to step up and take on that work unpaid. We never accepted the narrative, put forward by the Conservative-led government when they abolished the Audit Commission in 2015, that so-called armchair auditors would emerge to serve that public function. On the contrary, the systematic and wide use of the public rights in the Local Audit and Accountability Act and the resulting lack of action from auditors have clearly shown the limits of citizen action.

Overall the local government accountability and scrutiny system demonstrates widespread failings, as stated clearly in a 2013 report by Transparency International:

> Here, a disturbing picture emerges, and one on which experts and interviewees were agreed. On the one hand, the conditions are present in which corruption is likely to thrive – low levels of transparency, poor external scrutiny, networks of cronyism, reluctance or lack of resource to investigate, outsourcing of public services, significant sums of money at play and perhaps a denial that corruption is an issue at all. On the other hand, the system of checks and balances that previously existed to limit corruption has been eroded or deliberately removed. These changes include the removal of independent public audit of local authorities, the withdrawal of a universal national code of conduct, the reduced capacity of the local press and a reduced potential scope to apply for freedom of information requests (Transparency International UK 2013).

Having encountered many of these problems in the work of Research for Action, we believe that LOBO loans are symptomatic of much wider issues around unaccountability and lack of regulation and enforcement in local government, as a direct result of central government policy.

LOBO loans

Most bank lending to local authorities is in the form of LOBO loans. These loans are very long-term and typically start with a fixed or variable interest rate. The lender has the option to propose a new rate at predetermined call periods. These can be every six months or five years. The borrower's option is to either accept the new rate or repay the loan in full. If the bank does not exercise its option, the council can only exit the loan early by paying an exit fee, which is entirely at the discretion of the bank and usually very high. At least 240 councils were sold LOBO loans by several UK and European banks. The earliest loans of this type were recorded in the 1980s, but there was a marked increase in LOBO borrowing in the early 2000s in the run-up to the financial crisis. There are different types of LOBO loans, ranging from relatively simple 'vanilla' products to complex 'inverse floaters', where the interest is inversely tied to benchmark rates.

After the first national media report into LOBO loans, the documentary 'How councils blow your millions', screened on Channel 4 in July 2015, a parliamentary inquiry was started. Giving evidence, former Barclays trader Rob Carver explained to the inquiry: 'The important point here is that the borrower has no option to exercise until the lender has exercised theirs. The economic value lies with the lender. They are not going to exercise their option unless it is favourable for them to do so' (Housing, Communities and Local Government Committee 2015). A written submission by treasury-management advice company Arlingclose states: 'So heads the lender wins and tails the borrower loses. Only if the coin lands on its edge every time, and rates remain broadly flat for decades, does the local authority win' (ibid.).

In the post-crash low-interest environment, banks have had no incentive to exercise their options and councils find themselves locked into punitively high interest rates for decades to come. However, it is inaccurate to understand LOBO loans purely in terms of the cost involved. A crucial part is the derivative risk they carry. As explained by CIPFA in a bulletin:

> A LOBO loan can be analysed in terms of its financial components, as follows:
>
> 1. a loan at a floating rate which reflects the lender's cost of capital, the credit risk of the borrower, and the lender's profit margin;

2. an interest rate swap converting the variable rate into a fixed rate;
3. a series of options, one for each option date; these are known as Bermudan swaptions.

LOBOs are inherently risky as a result of their embedded optionality ... Authorities considering LOBOs will need to review LOBO quotes over a period of time, and understand the way in which pricing is sensitive to both swap rates and option value. The value of options is highly sensitive to volatility in market (swap) rates. The more unsettled long-term interest rates are, the greater the value in the options, and the better the LOBO rate should be (CIPFA 2015).

The more frequent the call dates, the riskier the loan is, as it increases the probability of the option being called and thus the refinancing risk. This is reflected by the fact that the more options are included in the contract, the more valuable the package of options is to the bank. By signing the contract, the council is effectively selling derivatives to the bank in the form of options.

Why LOBO loans are illegitimate

Research for Action has evaluated the legitimacy of LOBO loans generally based on the terms of the contract and the origin of the loans. We also analysed Newham Council's LOBO loans regarding the human rights implications of the servicing of the loans. The latter was done by examining our findings about the way residents' rights were being neglected through cuts in services in light of several international human rights declarations and conventions. We argued that violations of the rights of Newham residents to housing, health, democracy, social security and adequate living, as well as violations of the rights of children and young people, were exacerbated by the continuing flow of interest payments to the financial sector in the time of such crisis.

Most arguments regarding the contract and the origin of the loans were based on evidence provided as part of the 2015 parliamentary inquiry. In brief, we consider LOBO loans to be illegitimate for the following reasons:

1. LOBO loan contracts could infringe the laws on public policy, as it is *ultra vires* for councils to borrow to speculate using taxpayers' money. They also contain grossly unfair clauses that create excessive

risk, which were undisclosed to councils, such as unreasonable notice times for when the options are called and excessive breakage fees.

2. Councils were encouraged to take out LOBO loans by central government following the reforms to the Housing Revenue Account undertaken by Her Majesty's Treasury and the interventions made by the Treasury on PWLB rates and repayment penalties.

3. LOBO loans result from an excessive power imbalance between too-big-to-fail banks and public institutions. They were used by banks to circumvent regulation on derivative sales. Brokers were incentivised by banks' high, undisclosed commissions to sell LOBO loans through making exorbitant profits on them. In doing so, banks and brokers not only abused information asymmetries with councils but were also involved in rigging the rates (LIBOR and ISDAfix) the loans were pegged to.

4. Treasury-management advisers, who are hired by councils to provide independent advice, recommended LOBO loans to councils while receiving commissions from brokers arranging the loans. Brokers in turn were being paid high fees by both the council and the banks, which is not standard brokerage industry practice.

5. Some council administrations committed actionable breaches when taking out LOBO loans, such as contravening national policies, borrowing from foreign banks without Treasury approval and not appropriately benchmarking the loans against PWLB debt. Councils are also destroying or restricting the access of councillors, journalists and residents to documents related to LOBO loans.

What has been and can be done

When Research for Action published its report in 2018, Newham Council had recently changed leadership. The new mayor, Rokhsana Fiaz, had been a vocal opponent of LOBO loans as a backbench councillor and member of the Audit Board. Soon after she took office, the council announced legal action against Barclays and RBS banks. On the first anniversary of becoming the mayor, Fiaz announced Newham Council had terminated its LOBO loans with NatWest (formerly known as RBS). The bank had agreed to cancel six £25 million loans early with considerably low breakage fees, details of which were not released. Newham repaid the debt by borrowing from central government via the PWLB. According to the council, the renegotiation will save them £3.5 million per year for the 41 years remaining on the LOBO loans, with savings totalling £143 million. Through freedom of information requests, we found out that Newham was far from alone. At least £1 billion worth of LOBO loans sold by RBS to councils across the UK have been cancelled since the start of the citizen audit. The RBS loans were often some of the most toxic types of LOBO loans, with interest rates inversely pegged to benchmark rates, and thus, in the current low-interest-rate environment, councils were locked into paying rates up to, or close to, double digits. Most of the councils that have exited RBS loans have borrowed from PWLB to pay back the face value of the loans and an exit penalty averaging 36 per cent on the loans; we hold the data from such restructurings. This is far lower than the exit fees indicated by the fair value of the loans, which in some cases has been more than 100 per cent over the face value. The interest rate for PWLB borrowing averaged 2.61 per cent, compared to 8.53 per cent on inverse floaters and 4.09 per cent on vanilla LOBO loans.

In February 2019, seven councils announced they were suing Barclays over LOBO loans that the bank had sold them in the years 2005 to 2008. The loans' interest rates were pegged to LIBOR, a benchmark rate set by a group of London banks including Barclays. In 2012 it emerged that the banks had been manipulating the rate, and Barclays was fined £290 million. The local authorities – Leeds, Greater Manchester Combined Authority, Newcastle, North East Lincolnshire, Nottingham, Oldham and Sheffield – alleged that due to Barclays' role in the rate rigging, the banks knew customers would rely on LIBOR rates when deciding whether to enter into contracts. The councils are asking the court to cancel the loans without exit penalties and requesting restitution for sums in interest that they have already paid the bank. Overall, the seven councils' 49 LOBO loans with Barclays totalled £573 million. Barclays had already removed the options from its LOBO loans in 2016. However, the bank would have been unlikely to exercise its option in any case, and the move did not drive down the fair value that indicates the value of the loans to the banks; thus, it was unlikely to truly benefit councils. In 2021 the judge in the case ruled in Barclays' favour. Newham Council appealed and in 2022 the case was settled, with the Council saying it meant 'substantial savings' for Newham residents.

Central government has made no commitment to address LOBO loans; however, we have discovered that the NAO, government departments and CIPFA have been meeting with the councils' external auditors to discuss LOBO loans.

In 2018 one of the audit companies, Grant Thornton, refused to sign off the accounts of councils with complex 'inverse floater' LOBO loans before their accounting treatment was clarified. In response, CIPFA issued guidance on this.

Although LOBO loans – or at least their worst excesses – are being quietly wound down as a result of pressure, there are many unanswered questions about the role of government, auditors and regulators in the process of local government becoming a playing field for financial markets in the first place. The increasing reliance on the private sector for local government functions – and even the scrutiny function of the spending to deliver those functions – is not sustainable, as private companies are not set up to act in the public interest.

A piecemeal approach from auditors and arms-length bodies will not be enough without government intervention that ensures local government is properly funded and legislative change that reverses the financialisation of local government and ensures that financial risk is kept away from the delivery of public services. This is why Research for Action has called for not only the cancellation of LOBO loans without exit penalties but also the reversal of cuts and privatisation in local government, as well as an overhaul of regulation and of the audit regime. We also believe banks, brokers and treasury-management companies involved in selling LOBO loans to councils should be held responsible and made to compensate for the interest rates that have flown from the public sector to financial institutions.

The LOBO loan scandal also shows the severe shortcomings of the current privatised audit regime and the inadequacy of bringing the logic of finance into local government. Rather than short-term fixes, local government accountability needs a wholesale rethink on how to build active, democratic accountability and resident participation to ensure public funds are used in the public interest.

Notes

1   I use the term 'Spanish state' to include not only Spain but also Catalonia and other nations of the Spanish state.
2   This report was written in collaboration with Megan Waugh and includes work that stems from her ongoing PhD research project 'Public Accountability and the Outsourcing of Public Services' in the School of Geography, University of Leeds.

References

Alston, P., 2018. *Statement on Visit to the United Kingdom, by Professor Philip Alston, United Nations Special Rapporteur on Extreme Poverty and Human Rights*. United Nations Human Rights Office of the High Commissioner. 16 November 2018. Accessed 1 July 2021. https://www.ohchr.org/en/NewsEvents/Pages/DisplayNews.aspx?NewsID=23881.

Chartered Institute of Public Finance and Accountancy (CIPFA), 2015. *Treasury and Capital Management Panel Bulletin*. London: CIPFA. Accessed 19 January 2022. https://www.cipfa.org/-/media/files/policy-and-guidance/panels/treasury-and-capital-management/bulletins/tm-bulletin-final.pdf.

Citizen Debt Audit Platform, 2013. 'What the Spanish citizen debt audit platform (PACD) means by "citizen debt audit" and "illegitimate debt"', *Committee for the Abolition of Illegitimate Debt*. 21 June 2013. Accessed 1 July 2021. https://www.cadtm.org/What-the-Spanish-Citizen-Debt.

Communities and Local Government Committee, 20 July 2015. *Oral Evidence: Local councils and lender option, borrower option loans HC 353*. Accessed 11 February 2022. http://data.parliament.uk/writtenevidence/committeeevidence.svc/evidencedocument/housing-communities-and-local-government-committee/local-councils-and-lender-option-borrower-option-loans/oral/18808.html.

Malinen, F., 2015. 'Debt audits challenge the power of opaque finance', *openDemocracy*. 5 December 2015. Accessed 1 July 2021. https://www.opendemocracy.net/en/can-europe-make-it/debt-audits-challenge-power-of-opaque-finance/.

Makortoff, K., 2019a. 'RBS to wind down £1bn worth of contentious local council loans', *Guardian*. 23 March 2019. Accessed 1 July 2021. https://www.theguardian.com/business/2019/mar/23/rbs-to-wind-down-1bn-worth-of-contentious-local-council-loans.

Makortoff, K., 2019b. 'East London council claims victory with deal on NatWest loans', *Guardian*. 7 May 2019. Accessed 1 July 2021. https://www.theguardian.com/uk-news/2019/may/07/east-london-council-newham-claims-victory-deal-natwest-loans.

National Audit Office (NAO), 2018. *Financial Sustainability of Local Authorities 2018*. 8 March 2018. Accessed 1 July 2021. https://www.nao.org.uk/wp-content/uploads/2018/03/Financial-sustainabilty-of-local-authorites-2018.pdf.

National Audit Office (NAO), 2021. *Local Government Finance in the Pandemic*. 10 March 2021. Accessed 1 July 2021. https://www.nao.org.uk/wp-content/uploads/2020/08/Local-government-finance-in-the-pandemic.pdf.

Public Accounts Committee, 2018. *Financial Sustainability of Local Authorities*. House of Commons. 4 July 2018. Accessed 1 July 2021. https://publications.parliament.uk/pa/cm201719/cmselect/cmpubacc/970/970.pdf.

Research for Action, 2018a. 'Debt and democracy in Newham – A citizen audit of LOBO debt'. 4 December 2018. Accessed 19 January 2022. https://researchforaction.uk/debt-and-democracy-in-newham-a-citizen-audit-of-lobo-debt.

Research for Action, 2018b. 'Cuts and contempt – Experiences of austerity and council democracy in Newham'. 22 May 2018. Accessed 19 January 2022. https://researchforaction.uk/cuts-and-contempt-experiences-of-austerity-and-council-democracy-in-newham.

Research for Action, 2021. 'Democracy denied: Audit and accountability failure in local government'. 27 April 2021. Accessed 19 January 2022. https://researchforaction.uk/democracy-denied-audit-and-accountability-failure-in-local-government.

Transparency International UK, 2013. 'Corruption in UK local government: The mounting risks'. Accessed 1 July 2021. https://www.transparency.org.uk/publications/corruption-uk-local-government-mounting-risks.

3

'Forgive us our debts': lending, borrowing and debt forgiveness in Christian perspective

Nathan Mladin

The origins of this chapter lie in a conference paper written and delivered in pre-Covid times.[1] Debt levels were problematically high then. Now, as the economic fallout of the coronavirus continues to unfold, they are significantly higher and likely to rise further as various support schemes introduced by the UK government – payment holidays on mortgages and council tax, the furlough scheme, etc. – are phased out. For this reason, the key argument of the original paper is today more apposite than ever: debt is never merely an 'economic issue', but a deeply moral and ineradicably social one as well. It should be conceived in neither amoral nor narrowly moralistic terms, but appraised within the nexus of the relationships it articulates, reinforces or adversely affects.

The chapter develops this insight by sketching the history of Christian social and political thought on debt, focusing in particular on the 'jubilee' tradition of debt cancellation. This is not to suggest that only the Christian tradition recognises the moral aspects of debt, let alone that Christians are the only ones working for economic justice. This would be both manifestly false and presumptuous. Rather, the purpose of this chapter is to show how a Christian vision for economic relations, particularly those involving lending and borrowing, can provide a strong foundation for people of faith or no faith when developing interventions and proposals that help to tackle crippling debt and create pathways towards flourishing lives and communities. While acknowledging that no free-floating 'Christian view on debt' exists, I note a set of core ethical concerns and priorities regarding debt relations that run through the tradition. Building on these, in the second half of the chapter I seek to show how Christian social teaching can help reframe and reform contemporary debt so that it honours human dignity, fosters relationships of mutual assistance and inclines towards the common good. The chapter ends with a series of recommendations for addressing problematic debt, focusing specifically on contemporary applications of the jubilee principles of debt forgiveness and cancellation.

Debt is a complex and ambivalent notion which straddles a variety of spheres of human activity and relationships – economic, political, social and interpersonal. The fact that lending and borrowing are never merely 'economic issues', but fundamentally relational, social and, therefore, moral ones as well, should be a truism. Alas, often it is not. Debt is too often seen in reductionist ways: either it is intrinsically amoral or it is moralistic and focuses entirely on the borrower and their responsibility. Perhaps the exception to this is the case of problem debt experienced by people on low or no income who end up trapped in a cycle of debt and poverty. We may recognise such situations as morally troubling, even 'immoral' – particularly if exploitative or predatory lending is in play.

The reasons for this malnourished moral imagination when it comes to debt are many, and are rooted deeply and intricately in the history of liberalism and capitalism. They are beyond the scope of this chapter. Instead, this chapter explores the Christian tradition of social thought, which provides ample resources – principles and moral priorities – to recover a moral imagination for debt and address the problematic features of our debt-heavy economies.

As a social practice, relationships are always at play when debt is in view. In Christian perspective, debt expresses the very nature of human beings as creatures defined by and made for relationships, with personal and communal obligations. Debt can reinforce reciprocal relationships and express mutual assistance between human beings when lending is personal and shades into gifting, in the context of proximate relationships. 'I am in your debt' or 'I owe them a debt of gratitude' are everyday phrases which suggest that reciprocity and obligation are intrinsic to healthy human relationships. This is 'good debt', which reflects our personhood and fosters relationships of healthy interdependence. But when lending is predatory and exploitative and the obligation of paying back becomes a crushing burden for the indebted, debt can also erode relationships.

Financial language and practice in Christian thought

Before looking at some of the key biblical teaching on debt, some general observations about theological and economic discourse in the Bible are in order. The Christian scriptures are filled with economic and financial language and imagery: reckoning, redemption, gift, restitution, pledge and debt all feature prominently in the biblical text. One of the key biblical templates for 'salvation', God's work of 'putting the world to rights', is liberation from debt slavery. Release from the oppressive grip of debt is a key thread that runs through the Bible, from the Book of Exodus in the Pentateuch to Jesus' life as narrated in the gospels. The language of debt is also central in many theological accounts of the significance of Jesus' death. Redemption, for example, speaks directly to the reality of a costly buy-back and release from bondage (Mark 10:45; Romans 6:21–3; Colossians 3:5–6). This intertwining of theological and economic language is to be expected, given the Christian faith's unequivocal affirmation of the goodness of the body and material life.

Lending and borrowing in the Old Testament

The founding story of ancient Israel centres on the liberation from debt slavery in Egypt of the Israelites. Following this liberation, Israel is given the Law or Torah to order its religious, political, social and economic life. Many of the detailed regulations and injunctions pertain to economic issues: the distribution and sale of the land, work, rest, pay and commercial transactions. Underpinning them is the principle that economic relations, including lending and borrowing, are embedded within and subservient to social relationships of trust, mutual obligation and assistance.

Israelite families had an equal stake in the land. At this time and in this place, this was a deeply countercultural arrangement. Old Testament scholar Christopher J. Wright notes that in Canaan the land was owned by kings and their nobles, with the majority of people living as tax-paying tenant farmers (Wright 2004, 35 per cent).[2] For Israelites, the land was to be received as a gift to be stewarded on behalf of Yahweh, its only rightful owner (Leviticus 25:23). It could not be sold in perpetuity as a freehold: instead, it was limited to a maximum of 50 years as a leasehold contract. For the Israelite, the land was a fundamental means of subsistence and the basis of participating actively in the life of the community.

Lending and borrowing were permitted in ancient Israel with the understanding that they expressed and strengthened bonds of reciprocity and mutual assistance. The Old Testament law in fact encouraged lending freely, particularly to the poor (Deuteronomy 15:7–8, 10), but interest on loans was forbidden when Israelites lent to each other (Exodus 22:25; Leviticus 25:36–7; Deuteronomy 23:19–20).[3] In an agrarian, subsistence economy, people would generally be forced into debt by circumstances, borrowing in the case of crop failure or animal sickness or death. In this context, the ban on interest was a structural provision to prevent the erosion of the borrower's agency and their exploitation by a lender, who could selfishly take advantage of the borrower's misfortunes. This is also seen in the strict regulation around pledges taken by creditors as security for loans. The injunctions to return a cloak by night-time (Exodus 22:26–7), not to take a millstone as a pledge (Deuteronomy 24:6) or not to breach the debtor's privacy for a pledge (Deuteronomy 24:10–11) were meant as protections for the indebted. Underwriting these regulations was the understanding that poor and rich alike have intrinsic and ineradicable worth and dignity as bearers of the 'image of God' (Genesis 1:27) and as members of the community, and are essentially related to one other, with responsibilities and obligations flowing from therein.

At the start of the 'Sabbath year', which was to occur every seven years, debts or loan principals were to be written off. Hebrew debt slaves or, more accurately, bonded servants were to be released (Deuteronomy 15:1–6, 12–18). Masters would be required to provide them with what could be described as 'start up capital' (Jacobson 2016, 222):[4] animals, grains and other produce to enable them to provide for themselves and resume a life of appropriate self-reliance through work (Deuteronomy 15:14). Although freed, these Hebrews were landless and of low social status. Many would have to hire themselves out as day labourers or work as tenant farmers for Israelite landowners (Wright 1984, 129–38, 193–201).[5]

Every 50 years, therefore after seven 'Sabbath years', the Israelites were commanded to celebrate the Year of Jubilee and 'proclaim liberty throughout the land to all its inhabitants' (Leviticus 25:8, 9). Apart from the cancellation of debts, which was to occur, as noted above, every seven years, the jubilee further entailed the return of the land to its original inheritors (vv. 10, 13–17) (Mills 2021, 2).[6]

Taken together, the Sabbath Years and jubilee regulations can be understood as a powerful set of socio-economic institutions designed to reset economic relations. Sabbath rules sought to prevent the rich landowners' indefinite exploitation of their landless, poorer brothers. The jubilee provisions aimed to 'preserve or restore the integrity, independence and property of Israelite households' (Wright 1984, 129–38, 193–201).[7] Together these regulations were meant to counter runaway inequality and the entrenchment of injustice (e.g. long-term enslavement) and maintain, as economist Paul Mills notes, a society 'where all had access to property and the means of production, debt-free, at least once during their adult lives (cf. Micah 4:4)' (Mills 2011).[8] They suggest, more generally, that debt should be temporary and every member of the community given a fresh start. Upholding and, where needed, restoring people's agency and ability to be self-reliant through work were key priorities of Old Testament legislation. Debt cancellation was an important means of achieving this.

Until recently, the general view was that the Jewish Jubilee was a utopian aspiration rather than something ever practised. Recent scholarship shows, however, that jubilee types of events, involving the cancellation of personal debts (agrarian debts and arrears), liberation of bond servants and return of land to its original owners, occurred regularly in the ancient Near East, from 2500 bc in Sumer to 1600 bc in Babylonia and its neighbours, then in Assyria in the first millennium bc (Hudson 2018, ix).[9] These 'jubilees' generally took place at the discretion of a new ruler taking to the throne, when building a new temple or after a war. They had a demonstrably positive role in preventing growing economic polarisation and restoring a degree of social stability. What was distinctive about ancient Israel was that it formalised and codified what had hitherto been merely arbitrary royal proclamations. Israel 'took the practice out of the hands of kings and placed it at the center of Mosaic Law', as economic historian Michael Hudson puts it (Hudson and Goodhart 2018, 3).[10] The jubilee became 'the defining act of Jewish post-exilic identity' (Hudson 2018, 208).[11] Rather than being utopian, then, the Sabbath Year and jubilee regulations 'can be seen as a more regular, frequent and predictable version of economic institutions with an historic track record, designed to mitigate impoverishment through debt and the concentration of landholding into creditor's hands' (Mills 2021, 5).[12]

Debt in the New Testament

Echoes of the Sabbath Year and jubilee are loud and clear in the New Testament. In Luke 4, Jesus inaugurates and frames his mission with the jubilee prophecy of Isaiah 61:

The Spirit of the Lord is upon me, because he has anointed me to bring good news to the poor. He has sent me to proclaim release to the captives and recovery of sight to the blind, to let the oppressed go free, to proclaim the year of the Lord's favour (vv. 18–19).

After reading it, Jesus makes the striking claim that the message had been fulfilled then and there. In other words, Jesus presented himself as the embodiment of jubilee, powerfully showing that liberation from oppression and freedom from enslaving debt are squarely within God's purpose for the world.

Throughout his life on earth, Jesus surrounded himself with, and lived among, the socially, politically and economically disempowered and excluded. In his teaching, he radicalised the regulations and injunctions of the Mosaic law. Intriguingly, he consistently addressed lenders rather than borrowers,[13] showing a keen awareness of the asymmetrical power relation between lender and borrower. He did not simply forbid the practice of interest within the community, but actively encouraged lending freely, especially to those in need (Matthew 5:42). This was to be a form of lending that shaded into gifting. Moreover, he asked creditors to lend 'expecting nothing in return' (Luke 6:34–5), being ready to lose their assets, and thus sharing the risks of potential loss associated with loans.

In what is undoubtedly the most famous prayer in the Christian tradition, the 'Lord's Prayer' (Matthew 6:9–13), we find the phrase that gives the title of this chapter: 'And forgive us our debts as we forgive those who are indebted to us.' The first thing to note is that 'forgive us our debts' is not to be taken as the plea of the indebted towards the creditor. Rather, the phrase turns on an important analogy between debt and sin. In the Bible, sin refers not simply to individual wrongdoing or 'transgression' but to a cosmic, corrupting and 'malevolent agency bent upon despoiling, imprisonment, and death – the utter undoing of God's purposes' (Rutledge 2015, 175).[14] In theological perspective, both sin and debt act as domineering, enslaving and ultimately deadly forces if they are not eliminated. The point made in the context of the Lord's Prayer is that lenders cannot request forgiveness from God, and therefore liberation from the enslaving power of sin, without forgiving those indebted to them. The prayer marries the spiritual with the economic in powerful ways and provides a strong ethical foundation for both an individual and social ethics of debt forgiveness.

It is fair to say that in a biblical perspective, debt forgiveness rather than repayment of debt is the higher ethic. The Bible does expect borrowers to repay loans where the terms are fair and freely accepted, and they are able to do so. Dishonesty and trickery are roundly condemned. But as we have seen, the Bible is also deeply attuned to unjust practices and structures that disadvantage or exploit the poor. Hence the institutional and regulatory frameworks set up to mitigate and restore justice.

Debt in Christian history

The group of Jesus followers that emerges at the end of his earthly life is what political theologian Luke Bretherton calls a countercultural 'Jubilee community'[15] (Bretherton 2015, 246) of equality and hospitality, where wealth, food and other goods are shared freely and openhandedly according to need (Acts 2:44–5). The prohibition on interest (or usury, as it was known before the term came to mean predatory or illegal levels of interest, as it does today) was maintained for much of Christian history. Christian theologians during the so-called Patristic Period (100–451 AD) often condemned interest that trapped the needy in poverty as incompatible with the Christian ethic of loving one's neighbour. They saw usury as a form of robbery and violence towards the poor. Medieval theologians followed a similar line, upholding and codifying the ban on usury and arguing forcefully against unlawful means of profiting. But they also began to distinguish between legitimate interest and usury. Such redefinitions took place in a world where new opportunities for trading were emerging and new financial and economic centres, like Florence, were established. The distinction between legitimate interest and usury also influenced debates during the Reformation, when merchant capitalism was slowly emerging from medieval forms of social and economic activity. Lending and borrowing increasingly enabled a growth in entrepreneurial and commercial activity. Attitudes to debt began to shift. The Swiss reformer Jean Calvin notably refused to condemn lending at interest, pointing to the Bible's own refusal to do so (Janz 2008, 262).[16] However, the reformers remained alert to the social dangers of usury, where risks would be pushed down on the most vulnerable. Calvin urged lending and borrowing for the common good, by which he meant that loans made to the poor should be interest-free and equitable, according to the principle of 'do to others as you would have them do unto you' (Janz 2008, 262).[17]

Building on the body of biblical and historical teaching on debt and interest, contemporary theologies of debt range from a complete dismissal of debt and debt finance, understanding this as a form of slavery and corrosive to relationships,[18] to a cautious acceptance of debt, given its ineradicably ambivalent nature.[19] If there is a polyphony of views within the Christian tradition when it comes to debt, there is also, to push the musical metaphor further, a principal melody, or *cantus firmus*. When thinking about debt and economic relations more broadly, the intrinsic worth and dignity of all people and their constitutive relationships are paramount. Furthermore, economic relations and practices are always to be in the service of social relations and the common life. In other words, the market was made for people, not people for the market. There is a particular concern for the poor and the marginalised. As we have seen, this is central to the Old Testament laws, but is also seen in Jesus' and the apostles' teaching. It is enshrined in the official social teaching of the Roman Catholic Church.[20] Furthermore, there is a clear recognition of not only individual wrongdoing but also the injustice that arises at institutional and systemic levels. Finally, there is a clear concern for the inclusion of all in a common life.

Starting from these principles and drawing on the summation of biblical teaching on debt, the next section delineates the contours of a moral framework for assessing contemporary debt.

A moral framework for debt

Good debt

The key thesis of this chapter, and indeed the report on which this is based, is that according to the Christian tradition, debt is never merely an economic or financial issue: it is an inherently relational and moral one as well. In itself, debt is neither amoral nor immoral, but morally ambivalent. It should be judged within the particularities of the economic system to which it contributes, the uses to which it is put and its relational impact. Christian teaching on debt is particularly concerned with the quality of relationships debt establishes and fosters: between lenders and borrowers, but also within the wider society that is affected directly or indirectly by debt. Where creditors and debtors are in relational proximity (e.g. credit unions) and where there is a measure of mutuality, the bonds established through debt can contribute to their flourishing and the flourishing of the communities to which they belong. Refusing to acknowledge debts or obligations to parents, to nature, to society, among others, and refusing the messy but authentically human practice of making and keeping promises are contrary to what Christians believe is our nature, as fundamentally relational beings. With reference to economic debt, risks and losses associated with lending and borrowing need to be shared fairly between the parties involved, rather than pushed completely onto the borrowers, if debt is to pass what we might call the relational test (see Montgomerie, chapter 6).

Bad debt

Too often debt is part of a dark story. It plays into consumer capitalism's hollow promise that more is always better, or is used as a tool of domination and control, as in the Western nations' treatment of so-called highly indebted poor countries (HIPCs). Debt gives more power to the lender, while pushing most risks and costs onto the borrower. Scripture is alert to the severity and potentially abusive nature of the penalties that often attach to debt. The Book of Proverbs in the Hebrew Bible puts it strikingly: 'Do not be one of those who give pledges, who become surety for debts. If you have nothing with which to pay, why should your bed be taken from under you?' (Prov. 22:26–7). The risk, as the passage makes clear, is not only financial loss but also complete disenfranchisement. It is against such grim scenarios that we see the logic and need for regulation that seeks to limit the power of the lender and protect borrowers against abuse and exploitation. Today this includes interest-rate capping and price capping in the rent-to-own market,[21] extending the repayment schedule at fixed interest rates in order to make debt more sustainable and reforming bailiff practices to prevent the abuse of vulnerable people trapped in debt.[22]

Christian teaching stresses individual financial responsibility, but, as noted earlier, it is alert to structural injustice and denounces the forces and systems that erode human agency, freedom and dignity. To say 'greed is bad' and 'live within your means' is to give fine moral advice. But it rings hollow if there is not a clear recognition of the structural forces at play that heavily condition individual behaviour and constrict freedom. These include precarious work arrangements (e.g. zero-hour contracts with few if any basic benefits) and pervasive marketing, not least in the area of consumer debt.

Debt forgiveness today

For many people, the ability to borrow is a matter of life and death. There are loans on which people's lives depend, but which borrowers are then unable to repay (e.g. payday loans). Problem debt can, and often does, lead to a loss of meaningful freedom akin to slavery. In this context it is worth noting again that, when debt undermines the dignity and agency of the indebted, it is not debt repayment at all costs but debt forgiveness that is the highest ethical imperative in the Christian tradition. This is because Christianity, despite the failures of its adherents, is at its core a religion of 'grace' and freedom, of second chances and fresh starts made possible through the transformative power of gift.

The upshot of all this is not that all existing debts should be forgiven or cancelled wholesale. A literal application of the Sabbath and jubilee laws on debt cancellation would be both unfeasible and unethical: unfeasible because most debt–credit relations in today's complex economies are heavily intermediated via financial institutions such as banks, insurance companies and pension funds, and unjust because a universal debt cancellation would likely involve a systematic abrogation of property law (Mills 2021, 7).[23]

The upshot, rather, is that as a society we should consider applying the principle of debt forgiveness more widely, especially with regard to the poorest. This suggestion has particular urgency against the backdrop of the UK's high levels of income and wealth inequality,[24] growing levels of in-work poverty[25] and 'precarity'[26] – long-term trends the Covid-19 pandemic and the economic responses to it have only reinforced.

The Sabbath and jubilee traditions sketched in this chapter provide the deep rooting and moral vision to nourish the various debt cancellation campaigns, existing policy and legal mechanisms and new proposals to break the power of debt over the vulnerable in our midst. These include, but are not limited to, the Jubilee Debt Campaign's call for the cancellation of unpayable household debt[27] and the 'Reset the Debt' campaign of UK churches and faith-based groups and charities, which calls for £5 billion of government grants to repay council tax, rent and utility arrears accrued by the poorest households during the Covid-19 pandemic.[28] Contemporary outworkings and partial applications of the Sabbath and jubilee principles of debt cancellation can also be discerned in personal bankruptcy procedures (see Spooner, chapter 5), individual voluntary arrangements (IVAs) and debt-relief orders.[29]

A notable expression of debt cancellation profoundly consonant with the ethical vision outlined in this chapter is RIP Medical Debt's entrepreneurial response to the crippling levels of medical debt in the United States (Himmelstein et al. 2009).[30] RIP Medical Debt buys distressed debts owed to medical institutions (e.g. hospitals and other medical practices) at a steep discount (up to 99 per cent), using donated funds. It then wipes them out, mitigating significant financial and mental distress for millions of people. Since 2014, RIP Medical Debt reports that it has eradicated almost $5 billion in medical debt, providing relief for almost three million individuals and families[31] (see also Powell and Edelstyn, chapter 8).

To conclude, it is clear that the social objectives and relational benefits of the ancient institutions of debt forgiveness – respect for the dignity and agency of all, social inclusion, cohesiveness and economic resilience – can be attained, if imperfectly, through modern means. But if there are difficulties with implementing the Sabbath and jubilee principles of debt cancellation today, beyond any strictly technical constrictions, the loss of relational proximity and the erosion of the bonds of trust and solidarity are surely at the root. In any society, these are as difficult to create and sustain as they are essential; tragically, they have been particularly weakened in our own.[32] If we wish to implement the principle of debt forgiveness more widely, in the ways suggested in this chapter and other parts of this volume (Malinen in chapter 2, Spooner in chapter 5 and Montgomerie in chapter 6), and move towards more relational forms of lending and borrowing,[33] we must strive to mend and strengthen these bonds. With this goal in mind, Christians and people of other faiths and none have ample room to join hands and work together.

Notes

1 This chapter is based on Mladin and Ridpath 2019.
2 Wright 2004, Kindle edition, location 35 per cent.
3 Charging interest on loans extended to foreigners was permitted. This may seem perplexing at first. Examined more closely, it can be taken as a realistic concern to maintain the integrity of a common life by mitigating the lender's risk that a foreign debtor might never return and deliberately default on the loan. This exception to the ban on interest can be seen as a means of levelling the playing field between Israel and its neighbouring nations which practised interest in commercial transactions (Deut. 15:3, 23:20; Lev. 25:39–54). On this reading, the exception shows the Bible's acknowledgement of the distinction between personal, or what we might call 'subsistence', loans and commercial loans; put in contemporary terms, this is the difference between a payday loan taken out to replace a broken fridge and a 'credit line' requested by a business to finance normal commercial activity, for example.
4 Jacobson 2016, 222.
5 Wright 1984, 129–38, 193–201.
6 Mills 2021, 2.
7 Wright 1984, 129–38, 193–201.
8 Mills 2011.
9 Hudson 2018, ix.
10 Hudson and Goodhart 2018, 1–25.
11 Hudson 2018, 208.
12 Mills 2021, 5.
13 The Bible also refers to the obligations of borrowers. See, for example, Psalm 37:21: 'The wicked borrow, and do not pay back, but the righteous are generous and keep giving' (New Revised Standard Version [NRSV] translation).

14 In the Bible, sin refers not simply to individual wrongdoing or 'transgressions' but to a cosmic, corrupting and 'malevolent agency bent upon despoiling, imprisonment, and death – the utter undoing of God's purposes'. See Rutledge 2015, 175.
15 Bretherton 2015, 246.
16 Calvin 2008, 262.
17 Calvin 2008, 263–4.
18 See, for example, the resources produced by the Jubilee Centre, a Christian think tank based in Cambridge, UK.
19 See Bretherton 2019, 323–58.
20 See *Compendium of the Social Doctrine of the Church* 2005, chapter 7: 'Economic Life'.
21 For more information on price capping, see Financial Conduct Authority 2019.
22 See Taking Control 2017.
23 Mills 2021, 7.
24 Office for National Statistics 2021.
25 Joseph Rowntree Foundation 2020.
26 Wallace-Stephens 2019, 9.
27 Jubilee Debt Campaign 2021.
28 Joint Public Issues Team 2020.
29 These have been revised to enable more heavily indebted households to find relief. See UK Government 2021.
30 Medical debt accounts for two-thirds of US personal bankruptcies. See Himmelstein et al. 2019.
31 RIP Medical Debt 2022.
32 See Yates 2021.
33 Credit unions in particular offer a compelling model of relational lending that can play an important part in addressing the urgent problem of post-Covid household debt (see Groombridge et al. and Malinen, chapter 2 in this volume). See also Hargaden and McIlroy 2021.

References

Bretherton, L. 2019. *Christ and the Common Life: Political theology and the case for democracy.* Grand Rapids, MI: Eerdmans.

Bretherton, L. 2015. *Resurrecting Democracy: Faith, citizenship, and the politics of a common life.* Cambridge: Cambridge University Press.

Calvin, J. 2008. 'Letter on usury'. In Denis R. Janz (ed.), *A Reformation Reader: Primary texts with introductions*, 2nd edition, 262–5. Minneapolis, MN: Fortress Press.

Cavanaugh, W. 2008. *Being Consumed: Economics and Christian desire.* Grand Rapids, MI: Eerdmans.

Compendium of the Social Doctrine of the Church. 2005. Accessed 19 August 2021. https://www.vatican.va/roman_curia/pontifical_councils/justpeace/documents/rc_pc_justpeace_doc_20060526_compendio-dott-soc_en.html.

Financial Conduct Authority. 2019. *Rent-to-own and Alternatives to High-Cost Credit: Feedback on CP18/12 and consultation on a price cap.* Accessed 17 August 2021. www.fca.org.uk/publications/consultation-papers/cp18-35-rent-own-alternatives-high-cost-credit-feedback-cp18-12-consultation-price-cap.

Hargaden, K., and McIlroy, D. 2021. 'Credit unions: Relational lending as one solution post-Covid household debt', *Jubilee Centre*. Accessed 19 August 2021. https://www.jubilee-centre.org/blog/credit-unions-relational-lending-as-one-solution-to-post-covid-household-debt.

Himmelstein, D. U., Thorne, D., Warren, E., Woolhandler, S. 2009. 'Medical bankruptcy in the United States, 2007: Results of a national study', *American Journal of Medicine* 122 (8). https://doi.org/10.1016/j.amjmed.2009.04.012.

Hudson, M., and Goodhart, C. 2018. 'Could/should Jubilee debt cancellations be reintroduced today? If not, what alternative measures of debt relief and redistribution might be possible?', *Economics* 12 (1). Accessed 19 August 2021. https://doi.org/10.5018/economics-ejournal.ja.2018-45.

Hudson, M. 2018. *...And Forgive Them Their Debts: Lending, foreclosure and redemption from Bronze Age finance to the Jubilee Year.* Dresden: ISLET-Verlag.

Jacobson, R. A. 2016. 'Oppression interrupted: The Sabbath and justice', *Word & World* 36 (3): 219–27.

Joint Public Issues Team. 2020. *Reset the Debt*, December 2020. Accessed 17 August 2021. https://resetthedebt.files.wordpress.com/2020/12/jpit-reset-the-debt-report-update-dec-2020-1.pdf.

Joseph Rowntree Foundation. 2020. 'UK poverty 2019/20: Work'. 7 February 2020. Accessed 21 January 2022. https://www.jrf.org.uk/report/uk-poverty-2019-20-work.

Jubilee Debt Campaign. 2021. 'UK household debt'. Accessed 17 August 2021. https://jubileedebt.org.uk/campaigns/end-the-debt-trap.

Mills, P. 2011. 'The great financial crisis: A biblical diagnosis', *Cambridge Papers* 20 (1). (March 2011). Accessed 19 August 2021. https://www.jubilee-centre.org/cambridge-papers/the-great-financial-crisis-a-biblical-diagnosis-by-paul-mills.

Mills, P. 2021. 'After the virus: Is it time for a debt "jubilee"?', *Cambridge Papers* 30 (1). Accessed 19 August 2021: https://www.jubilee-centre.org/cambridge-papers/after-the-virus.

Mladin, N., and Ridpath, B. 2019. *Forgive Us Our Debts: Lending and borrowing as if relationships matter*. London: Theos.

Office for National Statistics (ONS). 2021. 'Household income inequality, UK: Financial year ending 2020'. 21 January 2021. Accessed 21 January 2022. https://www.ons.gov.uk/peoplepopulationandcommunity/personalandhouseholdfinances/incomeandwealth/bulletins/householdincomeinequalityfinancial/financialyearending2020.

RIP Medical Debt. 2022. 'Our mission'. Accessed 21 January 2022. https://ripmedicaldebt.org/about/.

Rutledge, F. 2015. *Crucifixion: Understanding the death of Jesus Christ*. Grand Rapids, MI: Eerdmans.

Taking Control. 2017. *Taking Control: The need for fundamental bailiff reform*. Accessed 17 August 2021. https://www.bailiffreform.org/storage/app/media/Taking%20Control%20report%20March%202017.pdf.

Tanner, K. 2005. *Economy of Grace*. Minneapolis, MN: Fortress Press.

UK Government. 2021. 'Consultation outcome: Debt relief orders'. 9 June 2021. Accessed 17 August 2021. https://www.gov.uk/government/consultations/debt-relief-orders.

Wallace-Stephens, F. 2019. 'Economic insecurity: The case for a 21st century safety net'. London: RSA. Accessed 17 August 2021. https://www.thersa.org/globalassets/pdfs/reports/economic-insecurity-21st-century-safety-net-report.pdf.

Wright, C. J. 1984. 'What happened every seven years in Israel? Old Testament sabbatical institutions for land, debts and slaves', *Evangelical Quarterly* 56 (4): 193–201.

Wright, C. J. 2004. *Old Testament Ethics for the People of God*. Downers Grove, IL: InterVarsity Press.

Yates, J. 2021. *Fractured: Why our societies are coming apart and how to put them back together*. Manchester, UK: HarperNorth.

4

Credit unions in the UK: promoting saving and dealing with debt

Martin Groombridge, in conversation with
Amy Horton and Christopher Harker

Credit unions are not-for-profit savings and loans co-operatives dedicated to promoting saving rather than borrowing. They also provide low-cost loans at times of need (London Capital Credit Union [LCCU] 2021). There are currently 280 credit unions in the UK, with a total of around 1,434,000 members and £1.8 billion in assets. These credit unions form part of the wider international co-operative movement, which can be found in 118 countries, with over 270 million members (LCCU 2021).

 This chapter examines how credit unions offer financial services based on a co-operative, rather than a profit-driven, ethos. The text is an edited version of a conversation with the chief executive of LCCU, Martin Groombridge. Martin became involved in the co-operative movement in 1979, when he saw a video about the Mondragon co-operative network in the Basque region. He was working in a factory, and the idea of electing your own bosses appealed. When he moved to London in 1995, he became directly involved with the credit union movement when officers of Rainbow Saver Credit Union, which was for members and staff of the Co-operative Retail Services, asked him, as an experienced co-operator, to investigate an alleged fraud. After resolving the case, he joined the board and has been working with and for credit unions ever since. LCCU can claim to be the UK's oldest credit union, and it is now one of the largest and fastest growing.

London Capital Credit Union

History and membership in the London context

LCCU is an amalgamation of many long-standing credit unions across London. It traces its roots to the Islington Council Employees' Credit Union, and eventually merged with North West London Credit Union, which was made up of three different credit unions in Barnet, and the Radio Taxis Credit Union, which was specifically for drivers and staff of that co-operative network.

The oldest continuously trading credit union in the UK was Hornsey Co-operative Credit Union. This was founded informally in 1960 by a group of people from the Caribbean who were quite openly denied access to mainstream banking. Credit unions were common in their home countries, so they set one up informally. In 1962 it was registered as a friendly society and became the second registered credit union in the UK. The oldest – Wimbledon Credit Union – had been established a few weeks earlier by another group of Caribbean migrants. Wimbledon Credit Union failed after a few years, so since merging with Hornsey Co-operative Credit Union, LCCU is officially the longest-running credit union in the UK. The largest proportion of LCCU's members (46 per cent) continue to be people who identify as African, Caribbean or Black British (LCCU 2020, 8).

LCCU's membership has grown rapidly, from 1,736 people in 2010 to 14,914 people in 2020 (LCCU 2020, 4). Two-thirds of the membership is female, and the majority describe their ethnicity as something other than White (LCCU 2020, 8–9). Sixty-two per cent of members live in homes where the total household income is less than £30,000; 37 per cent of members describe themselves as single parents. Typically, members are impoverished, Black and female, fitting exactly the profile of the people most affected by financial exclusion.

Operating in London offers LCCU distinct opportunities in two ways. First, the density of population means that an advertisement on a bus will be seen by more people in London than anywhere else in the UK; in rural areas, it is much more difficult to reach people. Second, London has a real ethnic mix, and certain cultures have a greater awareness of credit unions. For example, if you are Kenyan or of Kenyan origin, you will probably know about credit unions. In Kenya, 90 out of every 100 Kenyan shillings held in a savings account are held in a credit union, according to a Kenyan credit union delegation who visited LCCU in 2018. In Kenya, banks are for big businesses and high-net-worth individuals, while credit unions are for ordinary people. If a Kenyan moves to the UK and sees a credit union, they will sign up. White English people often do not have that history, trust and knowledge of credit unions.

The financial exclusion and indebtedness of LCCU members

Members of LCCU are generally not well served by banks. A small number are not banked at all, while the majority are banked but not well served. They pay high fees for basic services and are heavily indebted. LCCU's main objective is prevention rather than cure: preventing indebtedness and encouraging more people to save.

While there is no data on the kinds of debts that people typically have when they join the credit union, it is estimated that about 40 per cent of members borrow within six months of joining. These members have sizeable debts, which in this context means £3,000 to £4,000 or more. This debt is generally in the form of unsecured credit card debts and payday loans, as well as mortgage arrears.

Of the people that come to LCCU for loans, it is estimated that at least half are running overdrafts on a regular basis. For years they have been running an overdraft, which in most cases used to be free. As of 2020, the Financial Conduct Authority (FCA) said that the banks were no longer allowed to charge overdraft fees and penalty charges for bounced standing orders. What the banks have done instead is introduce a standard 39.9 per cent annual percentage rate of interest (APR) on overdrafts. It appears on bank statements if you look carefully, but it never shows you a single payment. They have introduced daily fees: they are charging interest, and it doesn't look like much. £1.26 or £2.40. But when you calculate these costs for a full month, that is a huge amount of interest people have to pay. It is the law of unintended consequences. The regulators have changed the regulations and for-profit institutions have just found ways around it to overcharge people.

Partnership with local authorities

LCCU has worked very closely with local authorities and social housing providers. In the early stages, when LCCU was reliant on external funding, local authorities were essential. Money from the New Deal under the Labour government funded the Islington and City Credit Union, along with some smaller grants from the local authority and community trusts and funding from housing associations. When LCCU was extended to Haringey, the council provided an interest-free, subordinated loan of £750,000, and this sizeable sum allowed the union to grow. This has now been partially repaid and stands at £400,000. LCCU was growing at about 20 per cent per year during this period (2008–18). The loan was, and continues to be, essential to maintaining the necessary capital–asset base ratio. For most credit unions, state funding is a good way of generating investment capital.

Local authorities promote credit union services to residents and to their employees to varying degrees. Generally, local authorities will promote the credit union once, and that is it. The real engagement comes when members of the credit union within those local authorities invite LCCU to talk to a group of staff and recruit them. For instance, LCCU is currently working with Barnet Homes, which is the arm's-length housing management organisation of Barnet Council. Barnet Council is not supportive, but Barnet Homes is, because there are lots of LCCU members working there, particularly in the income team. It is in its interest to have residents who are financially sound, because then they can pay the rent. It promotes the credit union when it sends rent statements out or when it sends the major works bill schedule to leaseholders.

Currently, LCCU turns away local authority projects because the time spent monitoring and providing data is simply not worth it. That time is better spent delivering services to members.

Credit unions in the UK

A distinctive approach to credit

In the UK, co-operative banks, building societies and friendly societies have traditionally enabled poor people to save, borrow and pay bills. However, when de-mutualisation occurred and they introduced the short-term profit-maximisation motive, many of these organisations started to move away from providing services in order to increase their profit margins. That model seeks to concentrate wealth in the hands of a smaller number of people, while co-operatives seek to build wealth among the greatest number of people.

Credit unions are profit-making institutions, but they are not driven by profit maximisation or short-term shareholder value. Credit unions want to return profits back to their members in the form of dividends and savings or rebates on the interest paid on loans.

Crudely, the primary objective of a chief executive working for a commercial bank is to increase the short-term share price over the next 12 to 24 months. Any fall in that share price means that person's job is at risk. In contrast, credit unions can make short-term losses, because they take a longer-term view and invest in the future. For instance, LCCU made a sizeable loss last year because of a combination of heavy investment in information technology and a shrinking loan book due to the Covid-19 pandemic.[1] That loss has been clawed back in the current financial year.

Credit unions can invest in small and unprofitable loans, knowing that they will lose money. However, borrowers will tell their families about how good credit unions are. These family members will then borrow money to buy a car or a new kitchen, and the credit union will make a profit there. Later in life, the borrower who defaulted might have moved into a better-paying job. They will then borrow larger sums of money to renovate their house, which will generate a profit for the credit union.

Credit unions take the longer-term view, helping individuals at the time when it is most needed and investing for a future commercial opportunity. The key difference compared with commercial banks is that credit unions are not driven by short-term profit maximisation. LCCU could be more profitable if it introduced setup fees for loans, charged early payment penalties, varied interest rates part-way through loans or required people to take insurance on their loans. These are normal practices in mainstream financial services. However, in credit unions the people being charged are the members, and the members decide how it is run. The chief executive and all other staff are directly accountable to the customers.

Credit unions are vehicles for community wealth building

Credit unions and co-operatives hold their profits within the geographical area in which they work. The money is kept within the community. All profits go back to members. The profits might not be huge, but it is money that is spent in local communities, corner shops, the local pub or going to the local football match. It is not siphoned off to Cayman Island accounts or to the leafy suburbs of Surrey. LCCU keeps wealth in the poorer parts of London.

Credit unions also create jobs. LCCU is currently small, but very ambitious. It could grow to a scale where millions of pounds are returned to the local community. Across the UK, credit unions are collectively returning millions to the communities in which they are based. They redistribute wealth back to local populations.

Problems that credit unions address

Currently, the big problem for communities is irregular income, or the so-called 'gig economy': low and irregular pay, irregular hours, the constant shifting of employers as contracts change and people never starting to save enough for an adequate pension because they are not in a job long enough. That is a real problem for individuals and particularly for longer-term savings. Pensioner poverty is a real issue.

There is a need for better financial providers and services for poorer people. For example, Provident Finance has just withdrawn from the market. They are so-called home credit–doorstep lenders who offer cash loans. I remember being very rude to them once. But when my mother was alive, she said 'you would never have had a school uniform if it wasn't for Provident Finance'. Recent regulation has resulted in a lot of lenders who served the subprime market going bust. Some were terrible firms, but some were fulfilling a social mission. It leaves a gap for the credit unions, but the problem is that other financial institutions then start competing with credit unions. If you choose to fight them, it is cost-ineffective and there are lots of these dubious firms around.

LCCU is currently working with Nest Insight, which provides the state auto-enrolment pension, to look at ways to increase people's propensity to save for pensions. The idea is that people will save from their salary with the credit union. When people join an employer, they are automatically enrolled unless they opt out. This has been trialled in the United States and has been successful. You might set a savings target of £500. £20 a month come out of your salary. You can take it out anytime you want. However, once you reach £500, anything more than that goes into your pension. The idea is that not only do you have an emergency short-term pot if you need access to finance, but also you are encouraged to gradually build up longer-term savings for your pension. It is one thing being poor when you are younger. You have time to build a savings pot. However, when you are older, it is a bit late to start thinking about a pension.

Challenges for credit unions

Access to capital

Access to capital and capitalisation is critical, and a lack of it is a key barrier to development. The hoops LCCU has to jump through for £150,000 are silly; someone can get a mortgage for £400,000 with an awful lot less effort. People in the public sector often have a different idea about money from people working in the commercial sector. If you do a quick Google search for fintechs, you find fintech firms asking for a £100 million of capital. These are huge investments. The largest credit unions have received only £5 million. Local authorities think £5 million is a lot of money, and it is. However, in terms of business investment, it is not. If there was a £50 million pot, with the right regulation in place, with the proper capital investment – not free capital necessarily, but patient capital – then credit unions could achieve much more substantial growth and provide services that an awful lot of people are currently being overcharged for.

Common bond legislation limits the number of potential members

The key legislative obstacle for credit unions is the common bond – that is, the rules on who can join. Community credit unions' common bonds are restrictive. There is an artificial regulatory cap that limits membership of these credit unions to three million potential members, not actual members. However, the cap on membership is a real barrier, because credit unions do not have the scale to be able to run efficiently as a business. For example, LCCU cannot advertise on the television in the peak slot during *Coronation Street*, because the vast majority of people who saw that advert would not be able to access LCCU's services. LCCU cannot advertise in the *Evening Standard*, because it is not cost-effective. Unfair limits on common bonds are, I believe, a restriction of trade, as they limit consumer choice and potential growth of the not-for-profit sector in financial services.

The argument for limiting membership via the common bond is that credit unions have relatively light-touch regulation by the Prudential Regulation Authority and the FCA. Credit unions do not have large compliance departments like the banks do. If credit unions reached a certain size, then they would need much heavier regulation. This would be absolutely fine. Reputation in the markets is essential. It would make sense for LCCU to have a group of compliance officers if it reached that scale. The common bond is a restriction of trade and a barrier to entry in the financial services industry. It is specifically aimed at stopping co-operatives from entering the market. It would be different if it were capped at three million members, but it is capped at three million potential members. LCCU would love to be a London-wide credit union. It has pushed the boundary of the rules. Anybody who is a member of the unions Unison or Unite or of the Co-operative Group anywhere in Greater London can join LCCU.

It is important to note that there are three different types of credit unions: associational, which might be people who are members of a church or a trade union; industrial, which could be employees of British Airways or employees of Stagecoach Bus Company, for example; or community credit unions, where the limit on geographical coverage is based on population. Industrial credit unions do not have the same issue with limits to common bond, because they tend to work, by definition, among paid employees. This is less risky and more profitable: they are not serving people who are unemployed, and they are not generally serving lone parents.

Difficulties providing certain services because of size limitations

Credit unions are restricted in terms of the services they can provide due to their size. Some credit unions used to and still do offer mortgages. However, the regulation has really been tightened up to prevent large credit unions providing mortgages. There is a lot of regulation that stops credit unions moving into new areas of business that could potentially be useful – particularly motor finance. Motor finance is a specialist area which has high interest costs. If you are buying a new car and you are earning a good income, you can get interest-free credit. However, if you want a second-hand car, which is what most people have to do, then you cannot get interest-free finance. Credit unions are currently not allowed to enter that market. They can offer loans to somebody to buy a car, but they cannot secure that loan against the vehicle like motor vehicle finance providers do. In many countries, motor vehicle finance is the core business of credit unions. In the United States, it is over half of the volume of the loan business. It is a real barrier for credit unions in the UK, especially since it is an area where people are being overcharged for credit.

Credit unions are not operating and advertising their services effectively

Credit union advertising could also be more targeted and effective. Most credit unions advertise their highest interest rate, when the more obvious tactic is to advertise the typical interest rate, which is considerably lower; LCCU does this, but a lot of credit unions do not.

I am a member of another credit union. They keep writing to me, and it is certainly not targeted marketing. I have borrowed from them and they know my income, yet they are trying to offer me a £200 loan for the school holidays when I do not have children. Credit unions are not as astute as they could be. That largely comes down to the common bond membership cap and the limited economies of scale that are possible.

Recruiting staff can be difficult

It is challenging to attract the right people to work in the credit union sector. I am very ideologically committed to the ethical purpose of credit unions, so I accept a lower salary than I might do in other areas of financial services. I am reasonably well paid and cannot complain; however, it still seems clear to me that to attract people, credit unions need to have salaries that are at least competitive with comparable sectors, if not equal to them. They also need to provide a clear career structure.

Opportunities for credit unions

Digitisation of services

The major opportunity for credit unions is going to be with regard to digitalisation and online. Without access to precise figures, we know that in the last 12 months there has been a huge move towards using online services. I have started to do some of my shopping online, now that the Co-op has started offering this service. (I rarely shop anywhere else as a matter of ethical principle.)

There are big advantages to using digital services, and in the last 12 months LCCU has been able to significantly improve its online offering. This has helped to improve the speed of services like online banking. For example, people do not have to send us documentation, which has meant timescales are quicker. Currently about 71 per cent of all unsecured lending is done online. Credit unions make up only a very small part of that. Digitalisation is going to make credit unions more accessible to people. Credit unions are good at what they do: LCCU has a very high customer satisfaction rating. Assuming it can continue like that, digitalisation will allow the company to move back towards 20 per cent annual growth. All of LCCU's membership growth and business growth comes from word of mouth. There is only a very small marketing budget, so our marketing is mostly through giving customers what they want.

Relatively modest capital investment is needed from the state

The issue of capital investment in not-for-profits and patient capital needs to be addressed. Part of this is accepting losses where necessary: recently there has been an initiative called Fair4All Finance, which provided a sizeable grant to underwrite the cost of some of the bad debt that is directly related to people losing jobs through Covid-19.

There is a real need for a national social investment bank that is focused on co-operative investments. These investments should be done on a commercial basis but with patient capital. If you are going to invest £20 million in a credit union, you should expect it to become profitable in 10 years' time. That is the only way it can work. The capital has to be patient. There is a huge scope for that sort of thing, particularly if we want to invest in communities that are marginally profitable or would never generate the sort of profit levels that would attract private sector investment.

There is a huge market for credit unions. What is needed is the right people in place – the right board of directors – the right policies and the right capital availability to be able to ride the storm when the company is growing.

Changes to regulation on size

If I could meet with the regulator and wave a magic wand, the 'big ask' would be to change the regulations so that if there was a legitimate business case, credit unions could grow beyond three million potential members. The easiest way to do this would be to say that no credit union can have more than three million members unless it meets a different regulatory regime. That would create a huge opportunity, particularly in major conurbations. The Greater Liverpool region has dozens of different credit unions, as does London. Things can change. The three million cap on membership is very recent. Previously, it was one million people. When I first started working for credit unions, they were restricted to single estates within local authority boundaries.

Credit unions can build a more prosperous society

Prosperity is not necessarily about whether you are a homeowner or not, or whether your income is above a certain threshold. It is about whether you have enough to be able to make certain choices – the freedom and independence to choose what to have for dinner tonight, for instance. If what is in the fridge is not what I want, have I got enough money in my wallet to be able to go and buy something else? Not necessarily a huge dinner at an upmarket restaurant. Prosperity is not just about cash value. It is about independence and choice.

Prosperity is also linked to certain patterns of behaviour and your ability to make independent and educated choices. If you are stressed and dealing with a financial crisis all the time, you are not going to be in a mental state to make educated, informed choices. Or you are less likely to. It's about having a say in things as well, so that you can have some influence. If a credit union has a minimum loan sum and you need a smaller loan than that, then you should have influence over that situation. I think that is prosperity as well – the ability to influence things that affect you. Of course, any definition of prosperity should also include good health. The link between ill health and poverty is well established, and it is economically cost-effective to address poverty. Every person joining and using their local credit union plays another small part in reducing poverty caused by over-indebtedness. Readers can find their local credit union by going to https://www.findyourcreditunion.co.uk/.

Notes

1   Anecdotally, about half of the people who come to LCCU for a loan want to buy a car, go on holiday or visit family overseas. Many members have family overseas. In the last 18 months during the Covid-19 pandemic, these people have not been borrowing to visit their family overseas. They used to go home every five years, and they are no longer able to do that. This has had a huge impact on pushing down LCCU's lending.

References

LCCU. 2020. *Annual Report 2019–2020*. London: London Capital Credit Union. Accessed 18 August 2021. https://secureservercdn.net/160.153.137.218/bn8.ba5.myftpupload.com/wp-content/uploads/2021/02/LCCU-AR-2019-20.pdf.
LCCU. 2021. 'About Us'. Accessed 28 February 2022. https://www.credit-union.coop/about/.

Part 2
Rewriting the rules

5

Can bankruptcy relieve the crisis of household debt?

Joseph Spooner

What to do about all of this debt?

As developed economies suffer under the negative consequences of excessive household debt, a strong case has emerged for extensive debt-relief policies. This chapter argues that bankruptcy should be considered among such policies, as it holds the potential to act as a safety net of last resort against the risks inherent to a debt-dependent economy. A decade ago, it would have been inconceivable to think that the shock of the Global Financial Crisis would not have launched a fundamental restructuring of contemporary capitalism. In particular, it seemed inevitable that there would be a dramatic change in the role played by household debt in the economic order. Yet household debt levels in advanced economies like that of the UK remain at historically high levels. Even before the economic shock of the Covid-19 pandemic, debt-to-income ratios of 140 per cent were drastically above the levels of 80 per cent seen in the late 1980s (Bank of England 2017, 3). Certain studies show that the share of disposable household income spent on interest payments is now higher than before the financial crisis of 2007–8 (Gibbons 2016, 4). The Financial Conduct Authority (FCA) has uncovered widespread defaulting among credit card users, and over two million credit card accounts are categorised as being in 'persistent debt' (FCA 2015, 2016, 2017). In 2017, the Bank of England was forced to take action to address the growing risk that rising consumer debt posed to financial stability (Bank of England 2017). Aside from these forms of financial debt, problems have soared over the past decade in relation to essential obligations such as rent arrears and debts owed to central and local government (London Assembly, Economy Committee 2015; National Audit Office 2018; Spooner 2017). The Money and Pensions Service estimates that approximately eight million people in the UK are 'over-indebted' (Money Advice Service 2016). These conditions have been exacerbated throughout the pandemic, which has not only deepened debt problems for many households, but has done so in a dramatically unequal manner (Citizens Advice 2020).

Meanwhile, governing politicians in the UK seem to have spent a decade in denial about the dangers this position raises, instead taking pride in the fact that levels of debt have fallen slightly below the 2008 peak which preceded the greatest economic disaster in memory (House of Commons Treasury Committee 2018). This complacency is characteristic of the failure of lawmakers to learn lessons from the last great crisis and subsequent Great Recession, and to take decisive action to address excessive levels of household debt. Indeed, the austerity policies of the past decade have in many ways perpetuated and accelerated trends of ever-increasing household debt, with reductions in public debt often merely causing increases in private debt (Barba and Pivetti 2009; Blyth 2013, 152–77; Streeck 2014, 38–40). Politicians have continued to support an economic model that relies on high levels of debt to allow households to both make ends meet and carry out enough spending to keep the economy growing (Bank of England 2017, 14–15; Crouch 2009). When faced with increased household financial precarity, they have essentially continued to repeat their pre-crisis mantra of 'let them eat credit' (Rajan 2011, 21). Loans have been substituted for wages, with households reduced to borrowing as their living costs have risen and wage growth has seen its worst rate in two centuries (Resolution Foundation n.d.). The reduction in household incomes through cuts and caps on social welfare payments, as well as the reduction in public service provision, has also caused households to turn to debt, where once they received support from the welfare state[1] (Prasad 2012, chapter 9). As we consider how policy might respond to the challenges of Covid-19, the importance of reflection on these trends becomes clear.

This status quo of inaction and the continued dependence of our economy on households borrowing increasingly large sums is unsustainable and deeply problematic. High levels of household debt are increasingly recognised as contributing to problems of economic stagnation (International Monetary Fund [IMF] 2012, 2016), income inequality (Berisha and Meszaros 2017; Lucchino and Morelli 2012) and political unrest (Blyth and Matthijs 2017). Even mainstream economic policy institutions (such as the IMF, Bank of England and Bank for International Settlements [BIS]) have torn up the pre-crisis (Washington) consensus that wider 'access to credit' is essentially a good thing for households and the economy (Turner 2015, 99), and now increasingly recognise the dangers of high levels of household debt. This danger applies not only to heavily indebted households but also to the wider economy. Under the 'debt overhang' problem generated by high aggregate levels of household debt (BIS 2017, 48–9; Bunn and Rostom 2015; IMF 2012; Mian and Sufi 2014; World Bank 2013), the use of future household income to pay debts amassed in the past leaves less money available to circulate in the economy (Coco 2012, 48). It perhaps would also have been inconceivable in the credit-boom years of the mid-2000s that a body like the IMF might open a report with the following words:

> Although finance is generally believed to contribute to long-term economic growth, recent studies have shown that the growth benefits start declining when aggregate leverage is high . . . new empirical studies – as well as the recent experience from the global financial crisis – have shown that increases in private sector credit, including household debt, may raise the likelihood of a financial crisis and could lead to lower growth (IMF 2017, 53).

While some policy documents adopting this perspective have been reluctant to state this directly, recognition of the dangers of debt presents a pressing policy case for extensive household debt relief. We have sacrificed future resources in order to pay for past growth, and as Davies notes, 'the problem with viewing the future as territory to be plundered is that eventually we all have to live there' (Davies 2017, 22). We are now living through the consequences of excessive past borrowing, and to free ourselves, we must not only restructure our economy to prevent future debt dependence but also remove much of this historic debt. The past decade has shown that this problem will not rectify itself – gradual 'de-leveraging', or paying down of the household debt stock, has been ineffective (unless, like the government of 2018, you find success in reducing household debt-to-income from 160 per cent to a 'mere' 140 per cent: House of Commons Treasury Committee 2018). Given theories and evidence of how a 'debt overhang' problem reduces economic growth and contributes to income inequality, the existing household debt burden might prevent the very growth in wages that would be necessary in order to de-leverage. The rebuilding of the post-Covid economy will require households to be in a position to contribute to present and future prosperity, rather than seeing their resources depleted in repaying debts incurred before and during the pandemic. Therefore, urgent action is needed to reduce existing debt levels through debt-relief measures.

This realisation places focus on bankruptcy law, since this is a societal institution unique in its cancellation of debt routinely and as of right. Bankruptcy laws take various forms in different legal systems. Even in England and Wales, a number of distinct procedures exist under the bankruptcy or 'personal insolvency' system.[2] The basic principle of bankruptcy law, however, is that a person who is unable to pay her debts ('insolvent') should receive a 'discharge' or cancellation of her debts at the end of a bankruptcy process (which in England and Wales lasts for one year), on complying with certain conditions (including making available to creditors any assets and income beyond those required for a reasonable standard of living). In this way, someone who has completed the bankruptcy process cannot be pursued further for his debts and receives a 'fresh start'. Household resources can be freed up for use in funding household living costs and returned to the Real Economy via household expenditure. Economic losses are redistributed away from average households and towards the financial sector, both reducing inequality and leaving more money in the pockets of those with the 'highest marginal propensity to consume' – i.e. low- and middle-income households who will spend any disposable income and offer the consumption needed for economic growth (Mian and Sufi 2014). Meanwhile, the strains of debt – psychological, emotional and with regard to health – can be lifted from struggling households (Davies, Montgomerie and Wallin n.d.; Porter 2011).

My book – *Bankruptcy: The case for relief in an economy of debt* – argues that in this way bankruptcy can operate as a social insurer of last resort, offering a safety net to desperate households and acting as an 'automatic stabiliser' to rebalance the wider economy. My book has two main aims. The first, which forms the focus of this chapter, addresses those who are interested in household debt-relief policies and illustrates why bankruptcy should be considered as a means of delivering such policies. It highlights the role of bankruptcy as an existing and well-established institution for the relief of debt. The second aspect of my book is more addressed towards bankruptcy policymakers, judges, administrators and lawyers. It aims to illustrate to custodians of the bankruptcy system why this area of law should dedicate itself firmly to a debt-relief objective, and to highlight how the law in its current state fails to do so effectively.

The case for bankruptcy

Even policymakers and authors who accept the dangers of excessive household debt sometimes fail to take the next step of advocating debt-relief policies. Even more so, they rarely acknowledge the significance of bankruptcy as a unique device for delivering debt relief routinely and as of right. Certain policymakers favouring debt-relief policies see 'no economy-wide tools available for large-scale debt restructuring' (Vlieghe 2016, 3). Other authors tend to look at current conditions as a time when 'all policy levers appear to be blocked' (Turner 2015, 12) and identify a minor role for debt write-downs without elaborating on how this might be achieved.[3] In his extensive history of debt, David Graeber wrote that in both historical and contemporary societies, states have

> insisted on *legislating around the edges*, softening the impact, eliminating obvious abuses like debt slavery, using the spoils of empire to throw all sorts of extra benefits at their poorer citizens . . . so as to keep them more or less afloat – but all in such a way as never to allow a challenge to the principle of debt itself (Graeber 2012, 390–1; emphasis added).

Responses to the financial crisis and the Great Recession appear to fit this description, as they have done little to reduce the existing household debt burden. In the UK, household-debt-policy responses included monetary measures to reduce interest rates, conduct of business regulation measures such as mortgage debt forbearance and rules establishing more responsible lending standards (Whittaker and Blacklock 2014, 22–30). Prudential regulatory measures were also established to improve financial stability, with the accompanying effect of maintaining the future supply of household debt at more sustainable levels (Bunn and Rostom 2015, 28–9). The government provided funding for money and debt advice services (House of Commons Treasury Committee 2018, 6), but without expanding the range of substantive assistance about which advice could be given. Access to bankruptcy was, for example, restricted through the austerity policies of the past decade (Spooner 2019, chapter 4). Some debt relief was provided through FCA redress schemes arising from misconduct in areas such as payday lending and payment protection insurance (PPI) markets (FCA 2014; Lomnicka 2017). This compensation was sector-specific and tied to proven cases of misconduct, however, rather than offering the generalised debt relief which present conditions seem to require. While many of these measures are laudable, it is possible to describe their collective effect as 'legislating around the edges', rather than tackling the principle of debt itself. All consider the current household debt burden as due and owing, and offer little to reduce this burden. One now wonders whether responses to the Covid-19 crisis will take more radical steps or be confined to temporary assistance measures such as eviction moratoria or debt 'payment holidays'.

Regulatory and market-based (*ex ante*) solutions

Some authors and policymakers focus on regulatory measures in addressing household debt, involving both prudential measures (relating to the solvency and stability of financial institutions) and conduct of business rules (relating to the treatment of customers by financial firms) (Bunn and Rostom 2015; IMF 2017). Certainly, these tools have an important role to play in reshaping our economic future and preventing crises of debt from rebuilding. These forms of *ex ante* regulation may indeed be more precise tools for ensuring responsible lending than the somewhat blunt tool of bankruptcy (which, for example, imposes losses on all lenders of an insolvent individual, whether responsible or not). These forward-looking measures leave the current household debt burden untouched, however, doing little if anything to reduce existing excessive household debt levels.

Other authors point to *contract design* as a means of addressing household debt problems, meaning that debt contracts could be written so that losses and gains are shared more equitably between lenders and borrowers (Mian and Sufi 2017). This might involve, for example, mortgage contracts providing that in the event of house-price increases, 'equity' gains are shared between the homeowner and the bank. Meanwhile, the contract could share losses between the two parties in the event of a fall in house prices. Contracts for unsecured debts might make the households' liability to repay contingent on certain economic conditions, meaning that flexibility is offered, for example, when an economic downturn arises. Problems with this approach arise from the fact that the failures in consumer credit markets that lead to over-indebtedness in the first place are likely to prevent such bargains from being struck organically in the marketplace. Bankruptcy scholars often argue that bankruptcy laws are necessary for the very reason that markets and the contracting process inevitably fail to produce the type of protection bankruptcy offers (Hallinan 1986). Even assuming (wrongly) that household borrowers might have the bargaining leverage to insert beneficial terms into their debt contracts, many of the macro-economic problems associated with excessive household debt are coordination problems. This means that a contract may be beneficial to an individual contracting household but disastrous when millions of those contracts are aggregated across an economy (Turner 2015, 164–6, 224–5). So, a mortgage contract involving no equity or risk sharing might look good to a homeowner hoping to benefit from house-price rises, but the widespread presence of this mentality may lead to excessive mortgage debt levels. Even if regulators were to impose such terms in the contracts of the banks they supervise, it is likely that any such measures would be sector-specific and suffer from the same limitations of *ex ante* regulations discussed above – they would do little to deal with debts arising from ongoing inflexible contracts signed in the past. Financially troubled households have multiple obligations under contracts with many creditors. If we rely on the terms of individual debtor–creditor contracts to address household debt problems, we may expect unrealistically that a financially struggling debtor will undertake a court litigation process for each contract. In contrast, the beauty of bankruptcy is that it does not examine underlying contracts but in one procedure simply draws a line in the sand and erases all included debts, irrespective of the terms under which they were incurred (Whitford 1994).

Monetary policy

Monetary policy could in theory address household debt problems, as central banks' reduction of interest rates makes de-leveraging more affordable for households. However, evidence from the past decade of 'ultra-loose monetary policy' (Turner 2015, 217) suggests that such measures have limited effect. Indeed, in law-and-economics scholarship, arguments are increasingly emerging to show the important contribution that measures such as bankruptcy law can make in a context in which central banks reach the 'zero lower bound' and can reduce interest rates no further (Furman 2017; Listokin 2017). Even where further interest-rate reductions are possible, evidence now suggests that they are 'likely to have asymmetrical effects in a high debt economy' – the reduction of rates may not cause heavily indebted households to spend (and so address the debt overhang problem) to the same degree that rate increases would cause them to cut consumption (Zabai 2017, 45). Further limitations arise from another asymmetry – indebted households may feel the effects of low interest rates to a much lesser degree than the investor class. Even in respect of mortgage borrowers, on average a period of over three years must pass before reductions in Bank of England interest rates are transmitted into lower monthly mortgage repayments (Bank Underground 2019). In respect of unsecured consumer credit, it appears that banks simply do not pass on interest-rate reductions to customers – interest rates on credit cards, overdrafts and personal loans saw little change in the years of 'ultra-loose monetary policy' following the financial crisis (Gibbons 2016). Meanwhile, high-end investors are sensitive to these low rates and in a position to profit from them, with the consequence that they may become incentivised to engage in highly leveraged financial speculation (Turner 2015, 218). This might have the perverse result of generating a further supply of household debt (as borrowers at low interest look for high-yield investment opportunities, including lending to households at increased interest rates). Not dissimilarly, the Bank of England's own research admits that quantitative easing benefitted the upper ends of the income distribution, offering little to the lower- and middle-income households who hold the highest marginal propensity to consume (i.e. society's chief spenders: Bank of England, 2012). Therefore, quantitative easing was another monetary policy with a limited ability to deal with the problem of debt overhang and its stagnating effects.

Fiscal policy and social transfers

I argue for a role for bankruptcy as a social insurance mechanism *of last resort*. From the perspective both of individuals and our wider society, a tragic state of affairs has arisen when bankruptcy is a solution. Bankruptcy is an incomplete substitute for robust social welfare protections and reasonable incomes, as evidenced in empirical studies of bankruptcy. Those who benefit most from bankruptcy appear to be those with reasonable incomes (Ben-Ishai 2005; Porter and Thorne 2006) and those with access to human and social capital (Palmer and Bhargava 2018). Research studies from the UK, US and Australia reach similar findings that bankruptcy offers less to debtors suffering from unemployment, ill health or persistently low incomes (Ali, O'Brien and Ramsay 2017; Atfield, Lindley and Orton 2016; Porter and Thorne 2006). Similarly, from a macro-economic perspective, social welfare transfers can act as 'automatic stabilisers' and effectively address macro-economic problems associated with household debt, particularly in times of economic downturn (IMF 2012, 13, 26).

The traditional social welfare system may be a more effective means than bankruptcy for addressing household debt problems. The politics of the welfare state, however, may limit its ability to fulfil this function. As noted above, despite the pressing need to address household debt, the trend over the post-crisis decade saw a retrenchment, rather than an expansion, of social welfare provision. Under the politics of austerity, 'automatic stabilisers' were removed rather than enhanced. Where the politics of social welfare provision have become intractable, the use of existing bankruptcy laws may offer an alternative form of automatic stabiliser and social safety net. For example, a recent IMF paper highlights the suitability of debt-relief-policy measures in 'economies with limited scope for expansionary macro-economic policies and in which the financial sector has already received government support' (IMF 2012, 27). At a time of austerity politics, bankruptcy offers a means of addressing household debt problems at low cost to the state. Once bankruptcy laws are 'on the books', they can automatically come into effect at times of economic downturn. This reduces the need to introduce novel bespoke policy solutions over the noise of polarised politics, which usually arises at times of crisis (Mian, Sufi and Trebbi 2014). In various countries, bankruptcy reforms have been introduced and supported by different constituencies across the Left–Right divide (Ramsay 2012b, 427). Bankruptcy also has the appeal of operating to internalise externalities arising in credit markets themselves. By imposing losses on creditors and so returning the social costs of over-indebtedness to the parties to the transactions that actually produce over-indebtedness, bankruptcy can claim to enhance market efficiency. It is a solution with redistributive potential, but which nonetheless is internal to the market itself. It therefore may offer attraction even to those who see classic tax-and-transfer redistributive policies as overly interventionist, productive of undesirable incentives or market distorting.

Market-based debt resolution measures

A number of organisations accept the merits of household debt-relief measures, but do not address bankruptcy. Instead, they advocate for various forms of standalone consensual debt-restructuring schemes to reduce debt burdens via creditor–debtor negotiation (Andritzky 2014; IMF 2012, 2016). In other words, experiences of crisis and recession have led a number of policy actors and commentators unfamiliar with bankruptcy to address the question of household debt relief for the first time, without regard for the experience of decades (if not centuries) of debt relief through bankruptcy. Dangers arise from the potential of this trend to ignore important lessons.

A key argument in my book is that evidence from bankruptcy law theory and practice highlights fatal limitations of 'market-based debt resolution' of the type advocated in these proposals (Spooner 2019, chapter 5). Contractual negotiations between household borrowers and large financial institutions are prone to failure, contributing to inefficient outcomes such as excessive debt, default and over-indebtedness. Negotiations between financial institutions and defaulting debtors – who have even fewer options and more limited resources than the average consumer – depart almost as completely as one could imagine from the classical economist's dream of perfect contracting in an efficient market. It seems implausible that bargaining under these terms could produce optimal outcomes, and empirical evidence from various bankruptcy systems bears this out.

The experience of consensual renegotiation under the individual voluntary arrangement (IVA) procedure in England and Wales has shown poorer outcomes for debtors than would have been reached through the statutorily imposed rules of the bankruptcy or debt relief order (DRO) procedures, with negative consequences from a public-policy perspective (Spooner 2019, 163–7). Studies from the Australian 'debt agreement' renegotiation procedure also show similarly poor outcomes for debtors (Chen, O'Brien and Ramsay 2018; Ramsay and Sim 2011). Academic researchers have concluded that the post-crisis mortgage consensual restructuring scheme introduced in the US – the Home Affordable Modification Program (HAMP) – was a 'dismal failure' (IMF 2012, 22–5; McCoy 2013; Porter 2011, 114–16; White 2009). Irish post-crisis reforms founded on voluntary renegotiation were widely accepted as ineffective. This even caused legislators to depart from their initial consensual model to introduce a procedure under which courts could impose debt-restructuring solutions in cases in which creditors have unreasonably refused a debtor's proposal (Spooner 2018). Prior experience across a number of countries suggests there are great advantages, therefore, in mandating desirable public-policy outcomes through bankruptcy, rather than waiting in vain for creditors to agree to the concessions necessary for such outcomes to arise.

A further chief advantage of bankruptcy is that it is an actually existing debt-relief mechanism. Severe political difficulties accompany any efforts to establish brand new debt-relief tools (Mian, Sufi and Trebbi 2014; Turner 2015, 226), both in terms of distributional conflict and the rhetorical and logical advocacy needed to explain why policy should depart from the seemingly self-evident idea that one must repay one's debts (Graeber 2012, 2–4). In contrast, bankruptcy laws have existed and developed over centuries, establishing well the principle of relieving debt in exchange for appropriate debtor scrutiny and sacrifice (Ramsay 2012a,

248; 2017, 6–7). This also means that the law has developed safeguards over many years to screen debtors and sanction misconduct (Spooner 2019, chapter 7). The robust legal mechanisms of the bankruptcy code offer a response to the classic cries of 'moral hazard' that tend to oppose any proposals for household debt relief (Levitin 2009). Policy might be better served by deploying this existing tool rather than expending valuable political capital in attempts to reinvent the wheel.

The limitations and potential of bankruptcy

Certainly, bankruptcy is not a perfect solution to the problem of excessive household debt, and it involves important limitations. Important authors argue that the seizure and sale of debtor assets typically occurring in bankruptcy could amount to a 'fire sale', with the negative effects of exacerbating falls in house prices, household wealth and consumption (Mian, Sufi and Trebbi 2014, 20; Turner 2015, 225). This criticism is less relevant to the current population of people entering bankruptcy and related procedures, who hold few if any assets that could contribute to a 'fire sale' (Spooner 2019, 102–5). It makes clear, however, that an expanded role for bankruptcy law must involve more reasonable means of dealing with mortgage debt that do not involve the mandatory sale of debtor homes. In this regard, bankruptcy scholars have shown how reforms to allow bankruptcy to deal with mortgage debt seem eminently possible (Levitin 2009). Related criticisms of bankruptcy include the facts that it may arrive too late and apply to only the most desperate and financially troubled of individuals (Mian, Sufi and Trebbi 2014, 20). Many people will feel the strain of debt burden, leading to their reduced social and economic participation and other social costs long before they become 'insolvent'. This suggests that bankruptcy as currently conceptualised and operating may not be sufficient to address the extent of our contemporary household debt burden, and that measures are necessary to alleviate debt among those households that are heavily leveraged but not yet insolvent. This may, however, simply raise a case for an expanded and reformed, and perhaps less punitive, bankruptcy system. We may need to accept that it is unnecessary for people to lose everything before they become eligible for debt relief. A related problem is that for obvious reasons bankruptcy is unloved, and continues to carry significant stigma (Ali, O'Brien and Ramsay 2015; Howell and Mason 2015; Sousa 2018). Any reimagining as a mass debt relief device may also require considerable rebranding.

Indeed, bankruptcy as it currently operates in England and Wales needs significant reform if it is to deliver the public-policy benefits associated with extensive household debt relief. Trends associated with neoliberalism and financialisation – including privatisation, fiscal consolidation and the marketisation of public services – have not only increased household debt difficulties and the need for debt relief. They have also driven bankruptcy policy and institutions in an opposite direction, reducing the availability and extent of debt relief. For example, the introduction of user fees and the effective privatisation of the personal insolvency system have pushed debtors from the public bankruptcy and DRO procedures into expensive IVAs of often dubious benefit (Spooner 2019, chapters 4–5). This pushes the law further from delivering its debt-relief aims. Similarly, increasingly aggressive government creditors have sought to shape the law to meet their own ends and to serve austerity policies of maximising debt recovery (Spooner 2019, chapter 6). Meanwhile, a preoccupation with individual responsibility, often through the lens of judgements issued upon consumers by (in the age of Big Data, increasingly all-seeing) markets, has led to overly punitive aspects in the law (Spooner 2019, chapter 7).

These problems must be overcome if bankruptcy is to fulfil its potential as a social insurance mechanism of last resort, and as a means of directly reducing the household debt burden. This chapter has aimed to highlight this potential and to show how bankruptcy might point the way towards a new economic order and a new politics of debt in illustrating the important role that the law plays in debt cancellation just as much as in debt enforcement. In this way, the existence of bankruptcy might offer a powerful and necessary challenge to the principle of debt itself.

Notes

1   Some examples of this trend can be highlighted among the austerity measures of recent years. Households have encountered debt problems when dealing with the six-week delay in payments built into the new 'Universal Credit' system of welfare payments (Drake 2017), while a more direct debt problem has been created by the conversion of the Support for Mortgage Interest (SMI) benefit into a loan scheme (Williams 2018).

2   Under the bankruptcy procedure, debtors receive a debt discharge after one year of payment of entry fees (£680), surrender of non-essential assets and contribution of non-essential income for a period of up to three years. Under the means-tested debt relief order (DRO), a debtor can similarly obtain a debt discharge after one year and need not contribute any income or assets to creditors – the procedure is designed for low-debt, low-income debtors who hold few assets. A reduced fee of £90 is payable by debtors entering the DRO procedure, who must obtain access through consultation with a debt advice agency. The number of bankruptcies and DROs has fallen in recent years, while there has been a rise in the number of individual voluntary arrangements (IVAs). This latter procedure does not guarantee any rights or outcomes to debtors, and instead is based on an insolvency practitioner (usually a commercial fee-charging IVA firm) negotiating

a debt resolution with a majority (75 per cent in value) of a debtor's creditors. An average IVA might involve a debtor making repayments to creditors (and paying fees to the intermediary firm) for a period of five to six years, often amounting to a repayment of approximately 40 per cent of her outstanding debt, with the remainder being written off. Recent years, however, have seen increases in the numbers of longer-term IVAs. For more, see Spooner (2019, chapters 4 and 5).

3   Turner suggests that 'reducing the value of debt through restructuring and writedowns . . . should certainly play a role', but his main suggestion is for 'fiat money' as a solution to the problem of lack of demand in the economy (Turner 2015).

References

Ali, P., O'Brien, L., and Ramsay, I. 2015. '"Short a few quid": Bankruptcy stigma in contemporary Australia', *University of New South Wales Law Journal* 38 (4): 1575–1613.

Ali, P., O'Brien, L., and Ramsay, I. 2017. 'Bankruptcy and debtor rehabilitation: An Australian empirical study', *Melbourne University Law Review* 40 (3): 688–737.

Andritzky, J. R. 2014. *Resolving Residential Mortgage Distress: Time to modify?* (IMF Working Paper WP/14/226). International Monetary Fund (IMF). Accessed 23 January 2022. http://www.imf.org/external/pubs/cat/longres.aspx?sk=42532.0.

Atfield, G., Lindley, R., and Orton, M. 2016. *Living with Debt after Advice.* Friends Provident: Institute for Employment Research, University of Warwick.

Bank for International Settlements. 2017. *The Global Economy: Maturing recoveries, turning financial cycles?* BIS Annual Economic Report. Accessed 23 January 2022. https://www.bis.org/publ/arpdf/ar2017e3.htm.

Bank of England. 2012. 'The distributional effects of asset purchases'. Accessed 23 January 2022. https://www.bankofengland.co.uk/-/media/boe/files/news/2012/july/the-distributional-effects-of-asset-purchases-paper.

Bank of England. 2017. *Financial Stability Report: June 2017* (No. 41). Bank of England.

Bank Underground. 2019. 'Bitesize: Fixing ideas – The slowing of interest-rate pass-through to mortgagors', *Bank Underground.* 27 September 2019. https://bankunderground.co.uk/2019/09/27/bitesize-fixing-ideas-the-slowing-of-interest-rate-pass-through-to-mortgagors/.

Barba, A., and Pivetti, M. 2009. 'Rising household debt: Its causes and macroeconomic implications – a long-period analysis', *Cambridge Journal of Economics* 33 (1): 113–37. https://doi.org/10.1093/cje/ben030.

Ben-Ishai, S. 2005. 'The gendered dimensions of social insurance for the non-poor in Canada', *Osgoode Hall Law Journal* 43: 289–320.

Berisha, E., and Meszaros, J. 2017. 'Household debt, economic conditions, and income inequality: A state level analysis', *The Social Science Journal* 54 (1): 93–101.

Blyth, M. 2013. *Austerity: The history of a dangerous idea.* Oxford: Oxford University Press.

Blyth, M., and Matthijs, M. 2017. 'Black swans, lame ducks, and the mystery of IPE's missing macroeconomy', *Review of International Political Economy* 24 (2): 203–31.

Bunn, P., and Rostom, M. 2015. *Household Debt and Spending in the UK* (No. 554; Staff Working Paper). Bank of England.

Chen, V., O'Brien, L., and Ramsay, I. 2018. 'An evaluation of debt agreements in Australia', *Monash University Law Review* 44 (1): 151–97.

Citizens Advice. 2020. 'Excess Debts: Who has fallen behind on their household bills due to coronavirus?' *Citizens Advice.* Accessed 6 April 2022. https://www.citizensadvice.org.uk/about-us/our-work/policy/policy-research-topics/debt-and-money-policy-research/excess-debts-who-has-fallen-behind-on-their-household-bills-due-to-coronavirus/.

Coco, L. 2012. 'Debtor's prison in the neoliberal state: Debtfare and the cultural logics of the bankruptcy abuse prevention and Consumer Protection Act of 2005', *California Western Law Review* 49 (1): 1–50.

Crouch, C. 2009. 'Privatised Keynesianism: An unacknowledged policy regime', *The British Journal of Politics & International Relations* 11 (3): 382–99.

Davies, W. 2017. 'The big mystique', *London Review of Books* (2 February 2017): 19–22.

Davies, W., Montgomerie, J., and Wallin, S. n.d. *Financial Melancholia: Mental health and indebtedness*. Accessed 16 February 2022. https://www.perc.org.uk/project_posts/financial-melancholia-mental-health-and-indebtedness/.

Drake, C. 2017. *Universal Credit and Debt*. Citizens Advice.

Financial Conduct Authority (FCA). 2014. 'Wonga to pay redress for unfair debt collection practices' [Press release]. Accessed 23 January 2022. https://www.fca.org.uk/news/press-releases/wonga-pay-redress-unfair-debt-collection-practices.

Financial Conduct Authority (FCA). 2015. *Credit Card Market Study: Interim report* (MS14/6.2). FCA.

Financial Conduct Authority (FCA). 2016. *Credit Card Market Study: Final findings report* (MS14/6.3). FCA.

Financial Conduct Authority (FCA). 2017. *Credit Card Market Study: Consultation on persistent debt and earlier intervention remedies* (CP17/10). FCA.

Furman, J. 2017. 'How lawyers can help macroeconomists in the wake of three major challenges keynote address', *Yale Journal on Regulation* 34: 709–42.

Gibbons, D. 2016. *Britain in the Red: Why we need action to help over-indebted households*. Centre for Responsible Credit (commissioned by TUC and Unison).

Graeber, D. 2012. *Debt: The first 5,000 years*. Brooklyn: Melville House.

Hallinan, C. G. 1986. 'The "fresh start" policy in consumer bankruptcy: A historical inventory and an interpretive theory', *University of Richmond Law Review* 21: 49.

House of Commons Treasury Committee. 2018. *Household Finances: Income, saving and debt: Government response to the committee's nineteenth report* (HC 1627).

Howell, N., and Mason, R. F. 2015. 'Reinforcing stigma or delivering a fresh start: Bankruptcy and future engagement in the workforce', *University of New South Wales Law Journal* 38 (4): 1529–74.

International Monetary Fund (IMF). 2012. 'Dealing with household debt'. In *World Economic Outlook 2012* (p. 1). IMF. Accessed 23 January 2022. http://www.imf.org/external/pubs/ft/weo/2012/01/pdf/c3.pdf.

International Monetary Fund (IMF). 2016. *Fiscal Monitor – Debt: Use it wisely* (Fiscal Monitor). IMF. Accessed 23 January 2022. https://www.imf.org/external/pubs/ft/fm/2016/02/fmindex.htm.

International Monetary Fund (IMF). 2017. 'Household debt and financial stability'. In *Global Financial Stability Report October 2017*. IMF.

Levitin, A. J. 2009. 'Resolving the foreclosure crisis: Modification of mortgages in bankruptcy', *Wisconsin Law Review* 2009: 565.

Listokin, Y. 2017. 'Law and macroeconomics: The law and economics of recessions', *Yale Journal on Regulation* 34: 791–856.

Lomnicka, E. Z. 2017. 'The impact of rule-making by financial services regulators on the common law: The lessons of PPI'. In L. Gullifer and S. Vogenauer (eds), *English and European Perspectives on Contract and Commercial Law: Essays in honour of Hugh Beale*, 51–66. Accessed 23 January 2022. https://kclpure.kcl.ac.uk/portal/en/publications/the-impact-of-rulemaking-by-financial-services-regulators-on-the-common-law-the-lessons-of-ppi(4a47b4e1-aa3f-434a-9d40-ba9776863203).html.

London Assembly, Economy Committee. 2015. *Final Demand: Personal problem debt in London*. Greater London Authority.

Lucchino, P., and Morelli, S. 2012. *Inequality, Debt and Growth*. Resolution Foundation Report. Accessed 23 January 2022. https://www.resolutionfoundation.org/app/uploads/2014/08/Final-Inequality-debt-and-growth.pdf.

McCoy, P. A. 2013. *The Home Mortgage Foreclosure Crisis: Lessons learned* (SSRN Scholarly Paper ID 2254672). Social Science Research Network. http://papers.ssrn.com/abstract=2254672.

Mian, A., and Sufi, A. 2014. *House of Debt: How they (and you) caused the Great Recession, and how we can prevent it from happening again*. Chicago, IL; London: University of Chicago Press.

Mian, A., and Sufi, A. 2017. 'The macroeconomic advantages of softening debt contracts', *Harvard Law and Policy Review* 11 (1): 11–30.

Mian, A., Sufi, A., and Trebbi, F. 2014. 'Resolving debt overhang: Political constraints in the aftermath of financial crises', *American Economic Journal: Macroeconomics* 6 (2): 1–28.

Money Advice Service. 2016. 'A picture of over-indebtedness'. Accessed 16 February 2022. https://www.google.com/url?sa=t&rct=j&q=&esrc=s&source=web&cd=&ved=2ahUKEwiMz5SO_oP2AhUkQkEAHcr2D5wQFnoECAIQAQ&url=https%3A%2F%2Fwww.maps.org.

uk%2Fwp-content%2Fuploads%2F2021%2F03%2Fa-picture-of-overindebtness.
pdf&usg=AOvVaw0NedK6tE_MvtkmGvFn6Nlb.

National Audit Office (NAO). 2018. 'Tackling problem debt'. Accessed 23 January 2022. https://
www.nao.org.uk/report/tackling-problem-debt/.

Palmer, L., and Bhargava, V. 2018. 'Forms of wealth associated with attaining peer group net
worth following bankruptcy', *Social Science Quarterly* 99 (1): 97–117.

Porter, K. 2011. 'The pretend solution: An empirical study of bankruptcy outcomes', *Texas Law
Review* 90: 103–62.

Porter, K., and Thorne, D. 2006. 'The failure of bankruptcy's fresh start', *Cornell Law Review* 92:
67–128.

Prasad, M. 2012. *Land of Too Much*. Cambridge, MA: Harvard University Press.

Rajan, R. G. 2011. *Fault Lines: How hidden fractures still threaten the world economy*. Princeton,
NJ: Princeton University Press.

Ramsay, I. 2012a. 'A tale of two debtors: Responding to the shock of over-indebtedness in France
and England – a story from the *Trente Piteuses*', *The Modern Law Review* 75 (2): 212–48.

Ramsay, I. 2012b. 'Between neo-liberalism and the social market: Approaches to debt adjustment
and consumer insolvency in the EU', *Journal of Consumer Policy* 35 (4): 421–41.

Ramsay, I. 2017. *Personal Insolvency in the 21st Century: A comparative analysis of the US and
Europe*. Oxford: Hart Publishing.

Ramsay, I., and Sim, C. 2011. *The Role and Use of Debt Agreements in Australian Personal Insolvency
Law* (SSRN Scholarly Paper ID 1942125). Social Science Research Network. http://papers.
ssrn.com/abstract=1942125.

Resolution Foundation. n.d. 'Public and family finances squeezes extended well into the 2020s by grim
Budget forecasts'. Accessed 16 February 2022. https://www.resolutionfoundation.org/press-releases/
public-and-family-finances-squeezes-extended-well-into-the-2020s-by-grim-budget-forecasts/.

Sousa, M. D. 2018. 'The persistence of bankruptcy stigma', *American Bankruptcy Institute Law
Review* 26: 217.

Spooner, J. 2017. 'Seeking shelter in personal insolvency law: Recession, eviction and
bankruptcy's social safety net', *Journal of Law and Society* 44 (3): 374–405.

Spooner, J. 2018. 'The quiet-loud-quiet politics of post-crisis consumer bankruptcy law: The case
of Ireland and the Troika', *Modern Law Review* 81 (5): 790–824.

Spooner, J. 2019. *Bankruptcy: The case for relief in an economy of debt*. Cambridge: Cambridge
University Press.

Streeck, W. 2014. *Buying Time: The delayed crisis of democratic capitalism*. New York: Verso
Books.

Turner, A. 2015. *Between Debt and the Devil: Money, credit, and fixing global finance*. Princeton,
NJ: Princeton University Press.

Vlieghe, G. 2016. *Debt, Demographics and the Distribution of Income: New challenges
for monetary policy –speech by Gertjan Vlieghe*. Bank of England. 18 January
2016, Department of Economics and Centre for Macroeconomics public lecture,
London School of Economics. https://www.bankofengland.co.uk/speech/2016/
debt-demographics-and-the-distribution-of-income-new-challenges-for-monetary-policy.

White, A. M. 2009. 'Deleveraging the American homeowner: The failure of 2008 voluntary
mortgage contract modifications', *Connecticut Law Review* 41: 1107.

Whitford, W. C. 1994. 'The ideal of individualized justice: Consumer bankruptcy as consumer
protection, and consumer protection in consumer bankruptcy', *American Bankruptcy Law
Journal* 68: 397.

Whittaker, M., and Blacklock, K. 2014. *Hangover Cure: Dealing with the household debt overhang
as interest rates rise*. Resolution Foundation Report.

Williams, S. 2018. 'Support for Mortgage Interest (SMI) – should you take this loan?' *Debt Camel*.
13 October 2018. Accessed 23 January 2022. https://debtcamel.co.uk/
smi-loan-help-mortgage/.

World Bank. 2013. *Report on the Treatment of the Insolvency of Natural Persons*. Accessed 23
January 2022. https://openknowledge.worldbank.org/handle/10986/17606.

Zabai, A. 2017. 'Household debt: Recent developments and challenges', *Bank for International
Settlements Quarterly Review* 2017 (December): 39.

6

Debt relief can finance prosperity: making the case for reducing the repayment burden on households

Johnna Montgomerie

Private, or household, debt is the policy puzzle of our time. Currently, debt is governed by national governments and international regulators using a deeply flawed moral economy logic. Credit is 'good' and is pumped into the monetary system as liquidity, allowing the entire macro-economy to function, yet debt is 'bad' when individuals have too much of it to keep up payments. Thus, the aim of monetary and fiscal policy is to find the Archimedean point, where enough good credit is produced to support the economy and bad stocks of debts are not created (see, for example, King 2016; Turner 2017). Unfortunately, the household debt stock has been growing steadily without any sign of abating in Anglo-America (understood here as the UK, the US, Australia and Canada), where household debt tied to residential housing has been the engine of macro-economic growth for decades (Hay 2011; Mian and Sufi 2014). In macro-economic terms, the primary driver of consumption is private debt (not wages). Rather, wages act as the guarantee of debt repayment revenues into the future (as outlined in Froud et al. 2009). This is important because household-debt contracts are peremptory claims on income, much like taxes on household budgets; more significantly, these monthly debt repayments have already been bundled together and sold on in global financial markets as assets.

Since the outbreak of the 2008 Global Financial Crisis (GFC), the Anglo-American and European countries have responded with 'unconventional' monetary policies. These policies are designed and implemented to stabilise volatile financial markets by making more credit available and purchasing assets (toxic debts); more significantly, they were combined with fiscal consolidation, or austerity, which removed state subsidies and services to households and communities. This dual movement between Treasury and central bank is significant as a policy challenge but beyond the scope of this chapter: instead, our focus is on how unconventional monetary policy can support prosperity rather than exacerbate debt-based inequality. For example, access to and wealth gains from residential housing are largely configured by the size of mortgage debt, age and location (Aalbers 2015; Christophers 2021; Montgomerie and Büdenbender 2014). Another example is access to higher education and income gains from it, which relate directly to age and amount of student debt required. A final example is when debt is used as a safety net to cope with a one-off emergency like the loss of a job or a severe illness; such scenarios often drive households into financial distress (Deville 2015; Montgomerie 2013; Roberts 2013; Soederberg 2013). After decades of promoting credit-driven growth in Anglo-America, for a growing number of people debt is a necessity, not an option. Debt was once an option, a choice, something that could be managed with buoyant incomes, and was even able to deliver wealth gains. Now, the necessity of debt eliminates prospects of ever being free from debt's obligations.

This conundrum is the reason why dealing with debts is key to generating prosperity. Financing prosperity requires dealing with household debts in a way that reduces the burden of debt obligation to improve the overall well-being of the economy and society. That means transforming the flawed moral economy of policymakers – which says that credit is good, as a profit source for lenders, but too much debt is bad, as a source of financial hardship for borrowers – while failing to acknowledge how credit and debt are related and configured by economic policymakers. A new set of priorities for governing the monetary system must be forged by addressing fundamental questions about the value of credit: what purpose does credit serve? How does credit generate well-being and distribute harm across society? What do we need credit for? Providing debt relief to households will support new norms to reorient the priorities of monetary governance.

The proposal put forward in this chapter is to use existing monetary measures to provide short-term debt relief that will be part of a wider reform of financial governance (part of the full proposal put forward in

Montgomerie 2019). Put simply, debt-relief measures involve *giving households access to 0 per cent refinancing on loans that they nominate, up to the value of the national median income for a period of 7 to 14 years.* If implemented, this would signal governance by a new moral economy in which the risks, rewards, wealth and harms of 'good' credit would be evenly shared between lenders and borrowers. As such, credit would be governed – by the Treasury, central banks and financial regulators – as an economic utility that operates for the benefit of the public. Credit generates well-being by facilitating economic activities that benefit society: it must be the servant, not the master, of the macro-economy.

An era of unconventional monetary policy

Unconventional monetary policy extends state funding to the financial sector, while austerity retrenches state funding to the household sector. In normal times, or non-crisis times, central banks limit monetary policy measures to monitoring inflation, adjusting interest rates and guiding credit. Unconventional monetary policy was first implemented in response to the Japanese economic crisis in the 1990s (Koo 2014). Since 2008, the United States, the United Kingdom, nations across Europe and the European Central Bank have all used 'unconventional' monetary measures to stave off the collapse of financial institutions as the result of market crisis (Braun 2018; Mattia, Lamperti and Mazzocchetti 2019; Young 2018). In simple terms, unconventional monetary policy involves two key features which are deployed differently in national contexts. Firstly, artificially low interest rates. Cutting interest rates is the most common response of the central bank to financial crisis. Unconventional monetary policy goes further, by accepting what is called a 'zero-bound' or 'negative' interest rate. Strange as this may sound, credit can have a negative interest rate if the interest rate is lower than the inflation rate. For example, in October 2017, the rate of inflation (consumer price inflation, or CPI) was 2.8 per cent and the base interest rate set by the Bank of England was 0.5 per cent (Organisation for Economic Co-operation and Development 2021a, 2021b). This monetary measure allows those institutions that are able to access short-term credit (the discount window facility) to accrue additional rents or income from financial assets, by borrowing government-issued debt at negative real rates and lending it on at much higher rates of interest. In the above example, there is an almost 2 per cent premium on billions of pounds borrowed, simply because inflation is that much higher than interest rates. Artificially low interest rates are an effective way to support the financial institutions able to purchase government debt directly from the Treasury.

The second element of unconventional monetary policy is quantitative easing (QE), which involves the Treasury transferring newly issued government debt or sovereign bonds (UK gilts or federal reserve bonds, for example) to the central bank. This is effectively a balance-sheet exercise, known as monetising debt, in which the central bank 'purchases' national debt, which is then channelled through credit and asset markets. QE is a 'powerful' signal of the central bank's support for its financial system (Best 2018; Braun 2016). A third element is central banks making large-scale asset purchases of, for example, troubled assets (toxic debts), corporate bonds or foreign currencies. This involves the central banks buying assets from the private sector using newly created reserves (or credit money). Whether central banks use newly issued credit to buy sovereign debt or assets, QE encompasses a wide range of different monetary measures that have sought to support financial institutions in the wake of the crisis in 2008 and in the face of persistent 'secular' stagnation ever since.

Inequality as an enduring problem of distribution

Acting as custodians of the national banking and global financial system, central banks succeeded in preventing a financial market crisis from becoming a total systemic collapse, but their measures have clearly failed to revive economic activity in ways that generate prosperity. This is primarily because unconventional monetary policy is deeply unequal in its structure (which is very clear when paired with austerity) and exacerbates wealth inequalities. For example, the Bank of England's initial monitoring analysis recognised that only the top 5 per cent of households benefitted from post-2008 asset purchases (Bank of England 2012). Similar studies have repeatedly shown that unconventional monetary policy has profoundly unequal distributional effects (Christophers 2020; Green and Lavery 2015; James 2020; Wood 2017). In other words, a very small group of rentiers (a term referring to those whose wealth is generated from rents or who act as rent-seeking agents) benefit from access to gains from unconventional monetary policy. In large part, intensifying inequality is down to who holds debt as an asset, compared to the levels of household indebtedness within the wider economy.

A simple understanding of how unconventional monetary policy exacerbates inequality can be gained by using interest rates and tracing how these translate into the terms of credit under which households borrow. Interest rates are set by the central bank and are the tool of monetary policy in normal and unconventional times. Central banks have kept interest rates artificially low since 2008 to ensure that there is plenty of credit flowing through the economic system.

Lenders, whether banks or other financial institutions, profit by exploiting the preferential rate of interest offered by the central bank and the market rates they charge on retail loans (a form of rent seeking). The 'terms of credit' for retail debt products are many percentage points higher than the near-zero-cost credit that is offered to banks in short-term lending, but banks also have far more credit-money reserves transferred directly from the central bank to be lent out. Lenders have near-zero cost and risk associated with the credit they lend to borrowers. But it does not stop there: lenders then sell on the anticipated revenues as a fixed-income asset (or securitised loan pool).

Lenders enjoy the dual advantage of charging considerably higher rates of interest on retail credit products held by the household sector and selling on these revenues as assets. Note that in the longest period of low interest rates, non-mortgage retail credit products have not become cheaper for borrowers: instead, they have become guaranteed revenues for lenders and debt-security holders. For example, credit card debts are 18–20 per cent, auto loans 4.5–6.5 per cent, lines of credit 3–6 per cent, overdraft facilities at major banks 33–50 per cent. Fringe financial products such as payday loans, logbook loans or doorstep lending charge interest in the thousands of percentages (1,000 per cent to 5,500 per cent). Admittedly, mortgage loans have interest rates that rise and fall in response to the central bank, but this is always to the advantage of the lender; however, more significantly, mortgage debt is a major driver of inequality in the UK and across Anglo-America. What matters here is recognising the difference (or spread) in the terms of credit, namely between central-bank-quoted interest rates charged on credit and retail credit prices – this demonstrates the baseline profitability of household credit products to lenders.

Another way of observing how unconventional monetary policy drives inequality is to examine how debt is distributed across society. Mortgage and consumer debts tend to be represented as aggregate measures or averages, but this obscures the reality of the unequal distributional outcomes of using debt to drive growth. For a very small number of households, debt is a source of wealth gains, either as leverage (or gearing, which refers to using debt to realise asset price gains) or as an asset holding. Some households owe no debts and have residential property as a non-financial asset. Another group of households owe different combinations of mortgage and non-mortgage debt. Finally, there are those without mortgages but with high-cost consumer credit. Therefore, there is an important distinction between households in which debt creates wealth gains and households in which debt obligations represent a peremptory claim on present-day income.

In practical terms, this dynamic plays out across Anglo-America as new forms of intergenerational and spatial inequalities. For example, in the UK, housing-based wealth gains accrue primarily to those aged over 50 and those residing in Greater London and the South-East region – whereas households aged under 50 or living elsewhere do not do as well, either because they are excluded from affordable housing, have more debt than wealth from residential housing, or have more debt than they can afford to sustain. However, it is not just access to housing. Debt is used in all aspects of everyday life in ways which affect certain groups. Think of student loans: only certain age groups were required to use loans to access higher education and/or pay rising tuition fees and costs associated with higher education. Also, consider how debt is used as a safety net to support households who have experienced unexpected hardship, like illness or job loss. Therefore, your age, where you live and your personal circumstances are much more important factors than, say, financial literacy in determining the degree to which debt benefits or harms the borrower.

In summary, the era of unconventional monetary policy has deeply intensified trajectories of wealth inequality, especially when combined with austerity measures in the post-2008 period. The unequal distribution of wealth gains, risk and insecurity consolidates economic stagnation and produces societal harms. Targeting household indebtedness – as the agent of stagnation, hardship and inequality – is a direct way of tackling these systemic issues.

Simple debt relief: offering a long-term refinancing operation to households

A simple and effective way of tackling household indebtedness – especially debts that are causing financial distress or hardship – is to refinance. Long-term refinancing operations (LTRO) are often used as a monetary policy tool to transmit interest-rate reductions to corporate borrowers during a market crisis. Put simply, LTRO allows the borrower to consolidate old loans (at higher interest rates) and swap them for new, lower-cost loans over a longer term. No new loans are issued; rather, existing loans are refinanced. LTRO works because the borrower pays lower debt-servicing costs on the same loan capital, giving the borrower access to present-day revenue/income to cope with crisis. For decades the LTRO has been a tried-and-tested first-response method used by central banks all over the world, but only to corporate or sovereign borrowers, not to 'retail' or household debts.

My proposal is very simple: extend LTRO to retail borrowers. *Give households access to 0 per cent refinancing of their problem debts for 7 to 14 years, up to the value of the national median income.* In 2021, in the UK, that would be equivalent to £29,000. Individuals could nominate debts up to that value for immediate 0 per cent refinancing for 7 years for non-mortgage debts and 14 years for mortgage debts. In the US, the value would be $65,700 and in Canada $65,000. These figures are just a starting point. Median income is a representative figure of income levels of the working population; here it acts as a benchmark of financial distress – borrowers carrying the entire value of the median income as debt stock, year-on-year. The scheme is financed in the same way all LTROs are financed: by credit guarantee from the central bank. Thus, it is administered as part of unconventional monetary policy. Most significantly, the LTRO provides relief to debtors by giving them more of their own income to spend. Think of the common argument in favour of tax cuts – the government is giving you back your money instead of taking it as tax revenue – the same applies for an LTRO, but it is the lender that takes a cut in interest revenue. Reducing the amount of interest paid on outstanding loans reduces the amount of monthly income dedicated to debt payments; this gives more present-day income to households to spend, save or invest. This small act of dealing with debts provides a new route to prosperity.

Importantly, the loans must be self-nominated by borrowers, not means-tested or nominated by lenders (who already do this via QE asset-purchase facilities). Giving individuals who are struggling the option to refinance any retail loan up to this value is essential for targeting problem or toxic debts in the system, which are largely unseen or unrecognised by financial authorities. As far as central banks and financial regulators are concerned, as long as debts are being serviced (i.e. monthly payments are being met), there is no problem debt. When payments are missed, each debt become part of the lender's pool of 'non-performing loans' (NPLs), dealt with as part of unconventional monetary policy. Up until now, the problem of the over-indebtedness of households has been monitored in a way that classifies types of debtors according to how well (or how badly) they are managing their portfolio of loans (Bryan, Taylor and Veliziotis

2011; Fondeville, Özdemir and Ward 2010). Typically, this is done by creating benchmarks, measuring degrees of financial fragility and classifying them into groups of debtors (see FCA 2014). The advantage of an LTRO is that borrowers can use it to target specific types of debts that cause the most harm to their household's balance sheet, without policymakers determining which households are worthy of debt write-down and which are not: all households have access to refinancing.

The benefit of using an LTRO method for writing down the costs of servicing debts is that it can target specific types of debt, namely those debts that cause the most serious economic distortions and are a source of harm in society. In contrast, targeting only problem debtors with specific amounts of debt runs the risk that an LTRO might be treated as an act of charity, not as an economic necessity required to end macro-economic debt dependence. It is better to target specific types of debt that are causing economic distortions, for example mortgage debts that fuel the housing crisis and, relatedly, intergenerational inequality.

As a tried-and-tested monetary policy measure, LTRO works, because it quickly transmits a fall in the rate of interest, or cost of credit, to borrowers. What is novel here is extending this to retail loans or household debts. An LTRO for households alters the terms of interest, length of loan and fees associated with lending, not the principal. Thus, it offers debt *relief*, rather than cancellation. Significantly, this redresses the stark hierarchy in the terms of credit created by rent seeking, by lowering the interest rate, not the principal of the loan. Lenders, regulators and central bankers want to believe that the high cost of credit is for short-term use by households, but this ignores how high-cost credit is used over the long term. For example, a very large proportion of credit card holders carry a balance for over five years, and many people rely regularly on current account overdrafts. Similarly, payday loans are 'rolled over' when a new loan is offered to cover the outstanding balance of the original loan. The length, or term, of a loan can be manipulated so as to make credit appear more affordable (the borrower pays a smaller monthly amount over a longer period), but at the same time it increases the overall cost, making credit more expensive because there are more payments.

Offering households an option to consolidate and refinance their high-cost consumer loans will rectify the huge distortions caused by growing indebtedness. Making long-term refinancing available to households will allow those with the highest exposure to problem (toxic) debt to consolidate loans of all kinds (each with different terms of credit). Debt relief will amplify throughout the entire economy, as borrowers have more present-day income available to spend, save, invest or pay higher taxes. This very simple measure of providing cheap credit can give relief to all manner of borrowers. Not only people already struggling in default, but all people servicing debts will be eligible. The process of application is the protection against fraud and abuse and will additionally provide new empirical evidence of indebtedness which can be analysed to provide much-needed insights into households' differentiated financial stability.

The opponents and advocates of debt relief for households

An LTRO for households is undoubtedly opposed by the global financial sector, despite it having been a willing recipient of the same monetary measures for decades. Indeed, this is its licence to produce money in the macro-economy, and it already enjoys considerable rents as a result of the institutional privilege granted by the Treasury and central bank. When it comes to household-debt relief, the global financial sector objects not as a lender (originator of loans) but as an asset-holder (holder of debt securities). This difference is important, because it reveals the power of the financial sector: global financial institutions are on both sides of the balance sheet. They have issued historically unknown levels of household liabilities, often directly subsidised by the central bank, because they are dependent on household income as interest payments on debt securities assets. Put in the simplest terms, refinancing household debt will be a 'haircut' to lenders, which means it will reduce the margin (or difference between the zero-bound interest rates and the hierarchy of terms of credit offered to consumers) that allows lenders to 'securitise' their outstanding loan pools on global financial markets. Anticipated future interest payments on household debts are the pipeline of revenue that feeds the global financial system monthly, but projections for the future are also tied to the stability of the financial system. Refinancing household debts will reduce the number of interest payments expected in the future (anticipated revenues), devaluing debt securities tied to those debts. Many pension funds, hedge funds, private equity funds and sovereign wealth funds own vast sums of debt securities as assets in their portfolio – as do all the financial institutions, national and global, that both issue and trade in household debt.

Admittedly, household-debt refinancing is a haircut. The case against an LTRO for households is the same as the case against any attempt to ask financial institutions to take a haircut: short-term losses will cause a huge financial crisis and 'banks will never lend again'. Such hyperbole is usually successful, because manias and panics are endemic to markets – although only in the short term. For example, this is why speculative runs trigger financial market crises, only for markets to rebound later. Furthermore, while banks might not lend in the short term, it is unfathomable that banks will not lend again – principally because it would mean that banks would forfeit their licence to create money by issuing loans to households. In more practical terms, the loss of anticipated revenue on household debts would contain losses within asset-class, household-debt products (while the global financial system has not proven resilient in containing losses, which is why the subprime mortgage crisis became a global financial crisis). Just as lenders benefit from publicly subsidised low-interest credit, an LTRO for households ensures that low-cost credit is passed on to borrowers. As the asset-holding financial sector benefits from publicly subsidised asset-purchase schemes, so too an LTRO for households ensures overall economic stability.

Advocates of debt relief for households have advanced similar proposals over the past decade. The use of the term 'debt jubilee' to refer to such policies first occurred in the late 1990s and early 2000s as a global policy response to remedy the economic hardship caused by the 'third world' debt of the 1980s. Debt jubilee for 'highly indebted poor countries' was a form of sovereign government debt cancellation designed to give relief to those countries worst affected by financial crises decades before. More recent, post-2008 policy proposals for a debt jubilee, or QE for the people, dovetail with the proposal made here. Economist Steve Keen (2012) advocates a 'Modern Debt Jubilee', which would give direct monetary financing to every individual taxpayer. He explains how existing double-entry bookkeeping practices between the central bank and private banks allow vast sums of debt to be created without reference to the underlying economic fundamentals; he then details how reverse engineering the same double-entry bookkeeping practices could cancel stocks of outstanding debt (Keen 2012, 2017).

A coalition of campaign organisations in the UK, led by Positive Money, advocates a 'quantitative easing for the people', which calls on the Bank of England to use policy tools to support a fairer economy that does not perpetuate inequality: 'Instead of pumping money into financial markets, it could be spent via the government into infrastructure, green technology, or as a direct boost to household finances' (Positive Money 2017). Writing in the *Guardian* newspaper, Mark Blyth, Eric Lonergan and Simon Wren-Lewis proposed the UK government 'legislates to empower the Bank with the ability to make payments directly to the household sector – direct monetary financing for households' (Blyth, Lonergan and Wren-Lewis 2015). A recent monograph by financial journalist Francis Coppola (2019) provides the most comprehensive explanation and justification of QE for the people as a necessary remedy for the 'failed experiment' of helicopter money for the financial sector. Chapter 3 outlines many different ways the central bank could deliver the same financial support to private households as it gives to private firms. However, there are deeper concerns expressed over using monetary policy to address distributional issues, which should be the role of government and the Treasury (Michell 2015; Toporowski 2010). This is important because central banks are technocratic, not democratic, institutions, so these proposals will only further empower unelected officials without democratic accountability in ways that impact citizens.

Governing credit as public utility

If the state is directly subsidising and underwriting the financial system, the effects need to benefit the wider public. At present, the benefits accrue as wealth holdings for a very small group. Prosperity is possible when credit is governed like a public utility rather than as an elite technocratic exercise. The governance of the national monetary system must recognise that risks associated with money creation are shared between the borrowers (who are registered citizens), the lenders (who administer the monetary system), the Treasury (which is the department of state) and the central bank (which governs the monetary system). An LTRO for household debts ensures that lenders carry some burden for generating the largest private-debt stock in history. Taking a haircut on high-cost credit and high-yield retail debt securities sends a signal that profits are not guaranteed forever. When borrowers become distressed, they can seek state-backed refinancing for 7 to 14 years. Currently, private debt is a lucrative profit centre taking up a larger and larger proportion of household incomes. More significantly, dependence on debt is the purveyor of perpetual financial crisis, which leads to the destruction of people's economic security and well-being. Debt must serve a useful purpose in building a better future – one that is sustainable over the long term.

Offering debt relief to households can be a remedy to secular stagnation or relief from the economic fallout of the Covid-19 pandemic. Giving households access to the equivalent of a 0 per cent balance transfer deal for outstanding debts equivalent to a year's median income would provide immediate relief for them and would spread the losses incurred by lenders over the long term. Currently, households use their income to service the huge stock of outstanding debt, creating a large and persistent drag on economic activity. Bail out households now, and banks will pay the costs later as 'anticipated' revenues from asset holdings. A debt write-down offers immediate relief to households by reducing the income-deduced costs of servicing debts. Securitising the LTRO loan pools would offer lenders the ability to spread their losses over the long term. Setting a closing date for the securitised pools (7 years for consumer debts and up to 14 years for mortgage-related debts) would create an end point for debt dependency, allowing lenders to unwind their investments in continued household indebtedness. A closing date for the securitised loan pool further signals an end to debt-dependent growth over the medium term. This ensures that refinancing existing debts does not simply reset the same conditions for another debt boom.

For credit to finance prosperity, retail household-debt products must once again become a small-margins business. Retail credit must be primarily used to fill the need for the kind of patient, long-term financing that can build prosperity. Deploying LTRO for households as a monetary tool will deter lenders from rent seeking on state-subsidised credit by charging higher terms of credit to retail consumers to preserve a lucrative profit centre.

Implementing fairness and equality in credit markets should not sound as radical as it does in today's debt-driven economy. A wider moral economy of central banking must now recognise that the new ease with which credit is created and passed on to lenders comes with a responsibility to eliminate rent seeking as a source of economic harm. If credit is that easy to create, then it can be eliminated as easily. Banks are given licence to create money by the Treasury and central bank, which becomes a flow of money in the economy using private-debt contracts. Moreover, those that hold claims on existing household debt as an asset class cannot have their anticipated gains put ahead of present-day economic hardship, because these conditions will soon create their own drag on the income available to make the payments.

Conclusion

Decades of debt-led growth has created an untenable situation: debt has been a driver of inequality and a series of crises followed by stagnation, which have not produced good economic outcomes for ever-growing segments of society. Now the economic shockwave of the Covid-19 pandemic threatens another round of unconventional monetary policy, coupled with austerity as the default response of the UK and other Anglo-American countries. Debt is not generating prosperity for the wider economy; instead, it is generating inequality to such an extent that it is harmful to society. My proposed LTRO for households will deploy state-backed credit to play a useful role in the economy and to improve citizens' prosperity. This will permit all borrowers to access the equivalent of a year's national median income for refinancing of capital at a 0 per cent interest rate for 7 to 14 years. A write-down of the household-debt stock will break the macro-entanglements of debt dependence by hiving off the debts that households are struggling with. Debt relief works by providing borrowers with more of their own income to save, spend or invest in the wider economy, creating an economic uplift with profound social benefits by addressing a key driver of inequality.

References

Aalbers, M. B. 2015. 'The Great Moderation, the Great Excess and the global housing crisis', *International Journal of Housing Policy* 15 (1): 43–60.

Bank of England. 2012. 'The distributional effects of asset purchases', Q3. Quarterly Bulletin. London: Bank of England. Accessed 1 March 2022. https://www.bankofengland.co.uk/-/media/boe/files/quarterly-bulletin/2012/the-distributional-effects-of-asset-purchases.pdf?la=en&hash=2B755A0984858DB90078EB78313CFD58F509F63A.

Best, J. 2018. 'The inflation game: Targets, practices and the social production of monetary credibility', *New Political Economy* 24 (5): 1–18. https://doi.org/10.1080/13563467.2018.1484714.

Blyth, M., Lonergan, E., and Wren-Lewis, S. 2015. 'Now the Bank of England needs to deliver QE for the people', *Guardian*, sec. Business. 21 May 2015. Accessed 24 January 2022. https://www.theguardian.com/business/economics-blog/2015/may/21/now-the-bank-of-england-needs-to-deliver-qe-for-the-people.

Braun, B. 2016. 'Speaking to the people? Money, trust, and central bank legitimacy in the age of quantitative easing', *Review of International Political Economy* 23 (6): 1064–92. https://doi.org/10.1080/09692290.2016.1252415.

Braun, B. 2018. 'Central bank planning? Unconventional monetary policy and the price of bending the yield curve'. In *Uncertain Futures: Imaginaries, Narratives, and Calculation in the Economy*, 194–216. Oxford: Oxford University Press.

Bryan, M., Taylor, M., and Veliziotis, M. 2011. *Over-indebtedness in Great Britain: An Analysis Using the Wealth and Assets Survey and Household Annual Debtors Survey. Report to the Department for Business, Innovation and Skills*. Institute for Social and Economic Research, University Of Essex. Accessed 24 January 2022. https://www.gov.uk/government/uploads/system/uploads/attachment_data/file/31897/11-747-over-indebtedness-in-great-britain-analysis.pdf.

Christophers, B. 2020. *Rentier Capitalism: Who owns the economy, and who pays for it?* London: Verso Books.

Christophers, B. 2021. 'A tale of two inequalities: Housing-wealth inequality and tenure inequality', *Environment and Planning A: Economy and Space* 53 (3): 573–94. https://doi.org/10.1177/0308518X19876946.

Coppola, F. 2019. *The Case For People's Quantitative Easing*, 1st edition. Medford, MA: Polity.

Deville, J. 2015. *Lived Economies of Default: Consumer credit, debt collection and the capture of affect*. Abingdon: Routledge.

Financial Conduct Authority. 2014. 'Consumer credit and consumers in vulnerable circumstances', Financial Conduct Authority. Accessed 24 January 2022. http://www.fca.org.uk/static/documents/research-papers/consumer-credit-customers-vulnerable-circumstances.pdf.

Fondeville, N., Özdemir, E., and Ward, T. 2010. 'Over-indebtedness: New evidence from the EU-SILC special module', European Commission Research Note 4. http://ec.europa.eu/social/BlobServlet?docId=6708&langId=en.

Froud, J., Johal, S., Montgomerie, J., and Williams, K. 2009. 'Escaping the tyranny of earned income? The failure of finance as social innovation', New Political Economy 15 (1): 147–64.

Green, J., and Lavery, S. 2015. 'The regressive recovery: Distribution, inequality and state power in Britain's post-crisis political economy', New Political Economy 20 (6): 894–923. https://doi.org/10.1080/13563467.2015.1041478.

Hay, C. 2011. 'Pathology without crisis? The strange demise of the Anglo-Liberal growth model', Government and Opposition 46 (1): 1–31.

James, D. 2020. 'Redistribution and indebtedness: A tale of two settings'. In Financialization: Relational Approaches, C. Hann and D. Kalb, 196–219. New York: Berghahn Books.

Keen, S. 2012. The Debtwatch Manifesto. Accessed 24 January 2022. http://keenomics.s3.amazonaws.com/debtdeflation_media/2012/01/TheDebtwatchManifesto.pdf.

Keen, S. 2017. Can We Avoid Another Financial Crisis? Malden, MA: Polity.

King, M. 2016. The End of Alchemy: Money, banking and the future of the global economy. New York: Little, Brown.

Koo, R. C. 2014. The Escape from Balance Sheet Recession and the QE Trap: A hazardous road for the world economy. Singapore: John Wiley & Sons.

Mattia, G., Lamperti, F., and Mazzocchetti, A. 2019. 'Unconventional monetary policy in the USA and in Europe'. In European Union: Post Crisis Challenges and Prospects for Growth, ed. Vasileios Vlachos and Aristidis Bitzenis, 37–61. Cham: Springer International Publishing. https://doi.org/10.1007/978-3-030-18103-1_3.

Mian, A., and Sufi, A. 2014. House of Debt: How they (and you) caused the Great Recession, and how we can prevent it from happening again. Chicago, IL; London: University of Chicago Press.

Michell, J. 2015. 'Corbyn and the Peoples' Bank of England', Jo Michell (blog). 5 August 2015. Accessed 24 January 2022. https://medium.com/@jomichell/corbyn-and-the-peoples-bank-of-england-755207f8de84.

Montgomerie, J. 2013. 'AMERICA'S DEBT SAFETY-NET', Public Administration 91 (4): 871–88.

Montgomerie, J. 2019. Should We Abolish Household Debts? Cambridge: Polity.

Montgomerie, J., and Büdenbender, M. 2014. 'Round the houses: Homeownership and failures of asset-based welfare in the United Kingdom', New Political Economy 20 (3): 386–405. https://doi.org/10.1080/13563467.2014.951429.

Organisation for Economic Co-operation and Development (OECD). 2021a. 'Interest rates (short-term) – OECD data'. Accessed 24 January 2022. https://www.oecd-ilibrary.org/finance-and-investment/short-term-interest-rates/indicator/english_2cc37d77-en?parentId=http%3A%2F%2Finstance.metastore.ingenta.com%2Fcontent%2Fthematicgrouping%2F86b91cb3-en.

Organisation for Economic Co-operation and Development (OECD). 2021b. 'Prices – Inflation (CPI) – OECD Data'. Accessed 24 January 2022. http://data.oecd.org/price/inflation-cpi.htm.

Positive Money. 2017. 'QE for people', Positive Money (blog). January 2017. Accessed 24 January 2022. https://positivemoney.org/what-we-do/qe-for-people/.

Roberts, A. 2013. 'Financing social reproduction: The gendered relations of debt and mortgage finance in twenty-first-century America', New Political Economy 18 (1): 21–42. https://doi.org/10.1080/13563467.2012.662951.

Soederberg, S. 2013. 'The US debtfare state and the credit card industry: Forging spaces of dispossession', Antipode 45 (2): 493–512. https://doi.org/10.1111/j.1467-8330.2012.01004.x.

Toporowski, J. 2010. Why the World Economy Needs a Financial Crash and Other Critical Essays on Finance and Financial Economics. London; New York: Anthem Press.

Turner, A. 2017. Between Debt and the Devil: Money, credit, and fixing global finance. Princeton, NJ: Princeton University Press.

Wood, J. D. G. 2017. 'The effects of the distribution of mortgage credit on the wage share: Varieties of residential capitalism compared', Comparative European Politics 15 (6): 819–47. https://doi.org/10.1057/s41295-016-0006-5.

Young, B. 2018. 'Financialization, unconventional monetary policy and gender inequality'. In Handbook on the International Political Economy of Gender, ed. J. Elias and A. Roberts, 241–51. Cheltenham, UK: Edward Elgar Publishing.

7

Mortgage debt and the housing affordability crisis

Josh Ryan-Collins

The house-price puzzle

House prices in the Global North appear to have defied economic gravity during the Covid-19 period. Massive falls in GDP due to repeated pandemic-induced lockdowns have been accompanied by near-record levels of house-price growth (*The Economist* 2021). The UK was no exception, experiencing a rise of over 10 per cent in annual house prices during the pandemic period (Office for National Statistics [ONS] 2021b) despite the greatest drop in national income – also around 10 per cent – in 300 years.

How do we explain this paradox? The standard explanation in the UK for the housing affordability crisis lies on the supply side. We are not building enough homes to meet rising demand from rising incomes and a growing population, especially in cities. An antiquated and inefficient planning system is often viewed as the key barrier (Barker 2004; Lyons 2014; Ministry of Housing, Communities and Local Government [MHCLG] 2020).

Yet the evidence casts doubt on these explanations. Approximately 90 per cent of planning applications in the UK are approved, with the latest data showing no drop-off during the pandemic period (MHCLG 2021b). Government household and housing stock data show that the UK actually has a *surplus* of dwelling relative to households (ONS 2021a;

MHCLG 2021a). This surplus grew by 70 per cent, from 660,000 to 1.12 million homes, between 1996 and 2018 (Mulheirn 2019).

Even if there are fundamental housing-supply constraints, the expansion of the housing stock appears to have a limited effect on housing affordability. Estimates of the sensitivity of UK house prices to increases in housing stock consistently show that a 1 per cent increase in housing stock delivers a reduction in house prices of between 1 and 2 per cent (MHCLG 2018). This implies that, with all else equal, expanding the housing stock by 20 per cent (approximately 5 million homes) over the next 20 years, roughly in line with current government projections, might bring down prices by 20 to 40 per cent (Mulheirn 2019). This contrasts with a 213 per cent increase in mean UK house prices between 2000 and 2021 (from £84,620 to £265,668: see ONS 2021b).

Furthermore, if supply really was the problem, we would expect housing rents to have risen at a faster rate than incomes in just the same way as house prices have. But in fact, rents have broadly tracked incomes, although the housing *cost* to income ratio (HCIR), which incorporates all housing costs (including council tax and utilities) and compares these to after-tax incomes on an annual basis, has risen from around 10 per cent in the early 1980s to 35 per cent now for private renters (Resolution Foundation 2017).

In recent decades, academics from a range of fields have begun to focus more on the demand for housing to find answers to the house-price puzzle. The demand for housing can be seen through its two economic functions: firstly as a consumption good (providing shelter) and secondly as a financial asset (providing returns over time).

As a consumption good, evidence suggests that in the UK, housing and land have a high 'income-elasticity of demand', meaning that as incomes rise, households spend more of their income on housing relative to other goods. One estimate across two UK cities found that a 10 per cent increase in incomes leads people to spend about 20 per cent more on space in houses and gardens, with homeowners having a higher income elasticity of demand than renters (Cheshire and Sheppard 1998). Another estimate found that between 1996 and 2001 the highest earners bought or rented accommodation that was 17m² per person larger on average than that of the lower earners (Boardman et al. 2005).

The idea that as incomes rise, people spend proportionately more on domestic space provides one explanation for the Covid-19 house-price conundrum. Although the UK economy as a whole went into recession, many middle- to higher-income households experienced an increase in savings, as their spending opportunities were curtailed for extended periods but their incomes were maintained (including those on furlough). They chose to use this additional income to pursue a 'race for space', purchasing larger homes or second homes (*The Economist* 2021; Partridge 2021). Undoubtedly, this was also influenced by an expectation that working from home would become more normalised in the post-pandemic period, as appears to be occurring.

At the same time, the demand for housing as a source of wealth – although hard to disentangle from consumption demand for primary residences – would appear to have significantly increased. The return on housing (made up of house-price appreciation and rental yields) has averaged around 7 per cent in high-income economies over the past 150 years. This is similar to stock prices but significantly less volatile, in particular since 1950 (Jordà et al. 2019), and is significantly higher than income and 'safe' assets such as government bonds. In the last 20 years, falling real (inflation-adjusted) interest rates have also contributed to making housing a more desirable asset by making rental yields relatively more attractive than savings or other 'safe' financial investments like government or corporate bonds.

These demand-side factors help us explain why building more homes may not address the housing affordability crisis. Wealthier households have strong incentives to increase their ownership of housing, whether for their own use or as a financial asset. They will be able to outcompete those on lower incomes with greater housing need in a lightly regulated housing market. The problem then becomes not so much the quantity of housing as its allocation across the population.

The role of debt and the financialisation of housing

Demand-side inequalities take on even greater importance when we consider the role of mortgage debt. The liberalisation of mortgage finance in advanced economies since the 1980s, coupled with financial innovations that have encouraged institutional investors to enter the housing market, have led to enormous increases of capital flowing into the housing sector at a rate far in excess of income growth or housing supply (Aalbers 2016; Gallent, Durrant and May 2017; Ryan-Collins 2018). In the UK, financial deregulation and liberalisation supported an increase in UK-based banks' mortgage lending from around 15 per cent of GDP in 1980 to 60 per cent by 2008, while lending to businesses increased from 10 per cent to just 30 per cent (Ryan-Collins, Lloyd and Macfarlane 2017, 117).

A rise in house prices relative to income creates even more demand for mortgage credit. Real estate's attractiveness as a form of collateral (being difficult to hide and increasing in value) gives banks confidence in continuing to meet this demand. This creates a positive feedback loop or 'housing–finance cycle' which can be hard to break out of without repercussions for financial stability and the wider economy (Ryan-Collins 2021a). This feedback cycle runs against standard economic theory, where an increase in the supply of goods, all else being equal, should eventually lead to a fall in prices. The explanation lies in the unique nature of housing as an economic commodity. Housing is a composite good, made up of the structure (the bricks and mortar) and the land underneath it. Location might be a better word than land, since in economic terms it is *where* a property is situated that determines its value more than anything else. Desirable locations – such as homes in job-rich cities, homes near green space or good schools – are *inherently limited* in supply. More and more credit and investment chasing a limited supply of housing is inevitably inflationary.

These dynamics considerably amplify the above-mentioned housing inequalities relating to income and wealth. The true demand for housing, in terms of purchasing power, is determined not by income but by income plus available mortgage credit – with mortgage loans usually being many times the income. Purchasers with higher incomes will also be considerably more attractive to banks as borrowers than those with greater housing need. Those who already own a property will be more likely to secure additional mortgage loans at lower interest rates for second homes or the purchase of larger properties.

The outcome is paradoxical. The mortgages that were supposed to enable more people to own property end up ramping up house prices to such an extent that homeownership declines. Indeed, recent empirical work finds a long-run negative correlation between increased mortgage debt and the level of homeownership in the Global North (Kohl 2018). But rather than pushing back on excessive demand for housing, government policies in the UK since the 1960s have generally supported demand, as the concept of the 'homeowning democracy' became embedded in the UK political economy. There has been a general shift away from subsidising the creation of homes and towards subsidising the demand for homeownership and private renting. Homeownership as a tenure and asset class has been favoured in terms of taxation, notably with the 1963 abolishment of imputed rent and the capital gains tax exemptions for primary residences which then became politically embedded as the rate of homeownership rose (Ryan-Collins, Lloyd and Macfarlane 2017). A range of mortgage subsidies have been introduced, including the ability to offset taxation against interest payments on investment properties (abolished in the early 2000s) and a range of schemes supporting first-time buyers. Recent evidence suggests these latter schemes had the perverse effect of increasing house prices as the increasing demand was capitalised into prices (Carozzi, Hilber and Yu 2019).

Additionally, government policy has created incentives for the purchase of second homes as investment properties. Most notably, the 1988 Housing Act made private renting much more attractive for investors by significantly strengthening landlords' grounds for repossession, abolishing fair rent appeals and reducing the minimum notice period for eviction from one year to six months (Leyshon and French 2009). In 1996, the introduction of 'buy-to-let' (BTL) mortgages led to a flood of new credit into the housing market, with increases of over 60 per cent each year until 2003. By 2008, BTL made up 11 per cent of total mortgage advances (Leyshon and French 2009, 443). Rising rents have led to huge increases in housing benefits being paid out to lower-income renters, which amounts to a significant government subsidy for landlords. Since most landlords come from the top 20 per cent of the income distribution, this further increases housing inequality.

Since the 2007–8 financial crisis, central banks have taken a closer interest in monitoring house prices and introduced macro-prudential policies aimed at restricting real estate credit to address 'systemic risks' across national economies (Cerutti, Claessens and Laeven 2017). Regulators have imposed limits on loan-to-value and loan-to-income ratios for mortgages and targeted buy-to-let and interest-only mortgages with some success in the UK, Australia, Switzerland, New Zealand and Hong Kong (Cerutti, Claessens and Laeven 2017; Kelly, McCann and O'Toole 2018). However, extraordinarily loose monetary policy has opposed such measures. Short-term interest rates have been reduced to the zero-lower bound, while quantitative easing (QE) programmes have driven down medium- and longer-term rates by hoovering up government bonds from capital markets. The hope was that this would lead investors to invest in more risky Real Economy assets such as debt and equity issued by companies. But the evidence suggests that rather than stimulating Real Economy growth, QE has led investors to seek out alternative 'safe' assets, with real estate, particularly in cities, being an attractive option (Moody's Analytics 2015). The 'wall of liquidity' created by QE catalysed a global search for higher-yielding but safe assets (Aalbers 2016). Landed property, particularly in rich cities, proved to be one of the most attractive assets for investors with global reach, not least because they could easily source borrowing, backed by property assets, at ultra-low interest rates from a banking sector which retained a strong preference for real estate. Property prices in global cities have 'synchronised', with price dynamics between these cities being closer to each other than those between the cities and regions in domestic hinterlands (Duca 2020). Although it is speculative buyers from home and abroad that usually target 'prime' (i.e. very expensive) properties, this raises prices across these cities and means they become unaffordable for those on middle incomes.

The Covid-19 pandemic saw these policy biases play out again with additional force. Fearing the collapse of the housing market in the face of the lockdown-induced recession, one of the first and most important fiscal stimuli provided by the Conservative government in the UK was a huge reduction in stamp duty, the main tax on primary residences. The subsidy, announced in July 2020, a few months after the first lockdown, meant there was no tax to pay at all on property purchases up to £500,000 in England and Northern Ireland. It ended in the spring of 2021. Alongside ultra-low interest rates, the stamp duty cut supported a record level of growth in mortgage credit. This expanded from £295 million in April 2020, as the first lockdown kicked in, to its highest-ever level of £11 billion by March 2021 (Ryan-Collins 2021b).

The question then arises of whether the UK is once again in a housing bubble and what damage its bursting would do to the economy and people's livelihoods. In the short term, the wider risk to the economy at the aggregate level from a fall in house prices looks less severe than in 2008. Household debt (including consumer debt) is lower relative to incomes, and so are interest rates on that debt. Alongside the savings that have been built up, this means that falls in people's housing wealth should have less of a negative impact on consumer spending. Banks are also much better capitalised than they were in 2007, meaning that a fall in the value of housing, which they hold as collateral against their mortgage loans, will be less likely to impact their lending activity.

In the medium term, the risks could be more severe. It is possible that the current inflation is due to bottlenecks in the post-Covid period, a position the Bank of England is currently taking (MoneyWeek 2021). However, it is possible to imagine scenarios whereby inflation becomes more sustained, particularly if it continues to rise in economies such as the US (where it is 7 per cent at the time of writing) and the eurozone, with which the UK has close trading links. Rising oil prices as global demand for energy or travel rebounds, or sharp increases in wages as the UK economy suffers ongoing shortages of labour due to Brexit-related issues, could also sustain high levels of inflation. That would put the Bank of England in a difficult position, since although average household debt-to-income ratios have fallen since the 2007–8 crisis, debt distribution across different socio-economic groups is far from equal. There is a 'long tail' of low-income households with high levels of debt – including unsecured debt – for whom even small increases in interest rates could make a material difference to disposable income and spending power (Resolution Foundation 2020). The Financial Conduct Authority (FCA) estimates that a quarter of all adults in the UK have low financial resilience, this being defined as having 'little capacity to withstand financial shocks' (FCA 2021). The government's promise of a state guarantee of mortgages worth 95 per cent of a property on homes worth up to £600,000 will increase the size of this vulnerable group.

Furthermore, the Bank of England's own research suggests that small rises in interest rates could contribute to falling house prices as property suddenly becomes less attractive to investors compared with safer assets like government bonds (Miles and Monro 2019). Thus, while a return of interest rates to a historical norm of 4 to 5 per cent seems highly unlikely, a rise to 2 per cent is more feasible but could still have damaging impacts on the economy, weakening consumer confidence at a time when the government may reduce spending or increase taxation due to worries about the public deficit.

Reforms to the UK housing market

What sorts of reforms could put the UK on the path to more affordable housing and a more stable and less real-estate-dependent economy? The UK is perhaps the canonical example of what has been described as 'residential capitalism' (Schwartz and Seabrooke 2008). Property wealth in the UK is 35 per cent of all wealth, while 91 per cent of all household debt is property debt. Once you become a property owner, rising house prices can be translated into cash via home-equity withdrawal, which has been permitted in the UK since the 1980s. This has propped up consumption, fuelling home renovations and other large purchases. In addition, many UK banks are only prepared to lend to smaller businesses if property (usually belonging to the business owner) is put up as collateral. All of this means that policies that would drastically reduce house prices would be economically and financially catastrophic and politically disastrous. A more gradual downward adjustment in house prices relative to increasing incomes is a much more attractive policy approach. There are three areas that policymakers should focus on.

Financial reform

At the national level, the Treasury and Bank of England need to find a way of incorporating house prices into the Bank's price-stability and financial-stability mandates. This will need to take account of regional variation, but the focus should be on bringing house prices back in line with incomes. Furthermore, financial policymakers in both central banks and ministries of finance should now have the confidence to regulate the quantity and allocation of credit for different purposes more explicitly. During their history, almost all advanced economies and many emerging economies employed formal and informal quantity-based credit regulation under various terms, including 'credit guidance', 'window guidance' and 'moral suasion' (Bezemer et al. 2021). The easiest way to introduce such a scheme might be to have some form of productive credit ratio, whereby a minimum ratio (e.g. 30 per cent) of a bank's assets supports non-financial firms (currently it is around 10 per cent on average in the UK). A gradual shift towards this kind of target would give banks the time to either reduce their mortgage lending or increase their business lending, depending on their preference.

Domestic regulations of this type would be more effective if they were complemented by supportive international regulation. International regulators, including the Bank for International Settlements and the International Monetary Fund, need to reverse the strong favouritism shown towards property lending in terms of capital and liquidity requirements. Regulations should support banks that are able to de-risk their loans via methods other than property-based collateral, most obviously by building up long-term relationships with non-financial businesses.

This brings us to structural changes to the banking system. A good model is Germany, where two-thirds of bank deposits are controlled by either co-operative or public savings banks, most of which are owned by regional or local people and/or businesses. These 'stakeholder banks' are more focused on business lending, do not have such stringent collateral requirements and devolve decision making to branches. They de-risk their loans not by requiring property as collateral but by building up strong and long-lasting relationships with, and an understanding of, the businesses they lend to (Beck et al. 2018). A second way of supporting non-collateralised lending for productive activity and priority infrastructure (including affordable housing) would be to create a sizeable UK State Investment Bank (Mazzucato and Macfarlane 2017) that could borrow at very cheap rates on financial markets, given that it would be underwritten by the government.

Tax reform

Reversing the fiscal favouritism towards homeownership and treating landed property in the same way as any other financial asset would be a logical step if we were to bring house prices back to levels closer to incomes. Council tax in England and Scotland has not been revalued since 1991, meaning a £150,000 home in Middlesbrough pays more than a £2.5 million mansion in Westminster (Ryan-Collins 2020). A recent study by the Resolution Foundation estimated that homeowners in the UK have enjoyed a £3 trillion windfall from soaring house prices, representing one-fifth of all UK wealth (Corlett and Leslie 2021). The report argued that levying capital gains tax at 28 per cent (as with other financial assets) would raise £11 billion a year and could have been an alternative to the £12 billion the Treasury will get from the increases in National Insurance contributions (a tax on employers and employees) announced in the October 2021 budget.

Another tax proposal, supported by economists from across the political spectrum, would be a tax on the increasing value of land, or land value tax (LVT), most famously proposed by the journalist and campaigner Henry George. This would involve an annual tax on the incremental increase in the unimproved market value of land that would fall upon the landowner. The advantage of this tax is that it would accurately capture the economic gains deriving from public and private investment in a location, such as a new school or better transport infrastructure, not due to the landowner's own efforts; in other words, the tax would capture economic rent for the public purse.

By attaching a cost to land ownership, LVT diminishes the incentive to buy land for speculative purposes to realise capital gains. Knowing that any increase in the value of a property would be taxed would lead to a shift towards households purchasing a house purely on the basis of its value as a place to live – i.e. as a consumption good – rather than as a financial asset. There would also be less incentive for developers to hoard undeveloped land. Such a tax would likely end the practice of 'land banking' or 'slow release' that, as the Letwin Review (2018) revealed, is a major issue in the UK. With rising land prices, developers are less incentivised to build and sell property efficiently, because the capital gains on their assets are rising, despite the shortage of housing the country faces.

There are major political challenges in implementing property taxes in most Western democracies, where homeownership and the idea of wealth generation from the home has become culturally entrenched.

There are genuine fairness issues in some cases, in particular where a household or individual is asset rich but cash poor, meaning a tax would significantly reduce their income. Any land tax should be introduced as part of a wider tax reform that would reduce other unpopular and regressive taxes such as income or sales taxes. Providing exemptions for low-income homeowners or allowing homeowners to defer payment until sale may reduce the unfairness critique (Cheshire and Hilber 2021). Homeowners could give up a percentage of their equity in the property each year that was not paid to the state, enabling the community to gain from any capital appreciation.

A major social housing programme

Is homeownership really the superior form of tenure from either an economic or social welfare perspective? There is little evidence that higher rates of homeownership support stronger economies. Rather, empirical studies have found that higher rates of unemployment correlate with high homeownership, as workforces are less mobile. High levels of homeownership reduce the efficiency of the distribution of labour and promote the interests of property owners in opposition to community development.

The UK used to have one of the largest public housing stocks in the developed world. A combination of mass privatisation via the Right to Buy and similar schemes, coupled with an insecure and low-quality rental market, has led to homeownership becoming the *de facto* superior tenure. This now needs to be reversed. Only a developer protected from the profit motive, such as the state itself, could ever have any incentive to produce houses at a rate that would lower the cost of housing overall in the area they are being built in. Building affordable housing to the highest environmental standards should be a key part of the Green New Deal, given the huge economic multiplier effects involved in construction at a large scale. Local authorities, perhaps supported by a National State Investment Bank, should be freed up to borrow in capital markets for socially rented housing that will provide a secure flow of income. Such a policy would also reduce emergency housing costs, which have been mounting since the austerity policies were introduced after 2010.

The private rented sector should be made as secure as possible, with long guaranteed tenancies, limitations on rent rises and strong tenants' rights. Government should take steps to boost the stock of non-market housing, including homes with social rents, community-led schemes and co-operatives, to ensure that different housing types and sizes are available in all tenures and to make housing supply less dependent on the volatile private market in land and homes. Finally, decent investment alternatives and secure pensions should be provided so that households are less prone to investing in the housing market to pay for their retirement or relying on it to fund their care in old age.

To ensure the costs of public housing are kept down, local authorities must be given compulsory purchase powers to buy sufficient land for entire new settlements. By capturing the planning gain for the public purse, the cost of the original land purchase can be made up and exceeded, with profits put into further upgrades to infrastructure. This is the model that was used successfully in the development of New Towns in the UK in the 1960s. This is standard practice in East Asian economies such as Singapore and South Korea and in European countries such as Germany and the Netherlands. Such powers enable the public sector to shape the land market in a way that prioritises housing's use value over its market value.

Conclusion

A decent and affordable home should be viewed as a human right, as advocated by the United Nations (United Nations Human Rights Council 2017). The commodification and financialisation of housing that has occurred over the past 30 years has left rich countries like the UK some distance from this goal. Political leaders must be brave enough to stand up to vested interests and make the case for housing to return to its primary function: of providing shelter rather than being a financial asset. As homeownership moves out of the reach of more and more young households and those of poorer people, this process should become easier. A key challenge will be de-linking our financial system and wider economy from the place we live in without causing financial havoc. Banks need to be weaned off their dependence on the housing market. Governments should be taking steps now to direct finance towards more productive ends, not least the creation of new housing and transport infrastructures that would boost economic growth and consumption but ease pressure on our cities. A gradual, managed rebalancing of house prices relative to income is required, with demand coming from investment and production, not off the back of rising asset prices and rising household indebtedness.

References

Aalbers, M. B. 2016. *The Financialization of Housing: A political economy approach*. London: Routledge.

Barker, K. 2004. *Review of Housing Supply: Delivering stability: Securing our future housing needs: Final report: Recommendations*. London: Stationery Office.

Beck, T., Degryse, H., De Haas, R., and Van Horen, N. 2018. 'When arm's length is too far: Relationship banking over the credit cycle', *Journal of Financial Economics* 127 (1): 174–96.

Bezemer, D., Ryan-Collins, J., van Lerven, F., and Zhang, L. 2021. 'Credit policy and the "debt shift" in advanced economies', *Socio-Economic Review*, mwab041, https://doi.org/10.1093/ser/mwab041.

Boardman, B., Darby, S., Killip, G., Hinnells, M., Jardine, C. N., Palmer, J., Sinden, G., Lane, K., Layberry, R. and Wright, A. 2005. *40% House*. Oxford: Environmental Change Institute, University of Oxford. Accessed 24 January 2022. https://www.eci.ox.ac.uk/research/energy/downloads/40house/40house.pdf.

Carozzi, F., Hilber, C. A., and Yu, X. 2019. *The Economic Impacts of Help to Buy*. London School of Economics, mimeo.

Cerutti, E., Claessens, S., and Laeven, L. 2017. 'The use and effectiveness of macroprudential policies: New evidence', *Journal of Financial Stability* 28: 203–24.

Cheshire, P., and Hilber, C. 2021. 'Home truths: Options for reforming residential property taxes in England', *Bright Blue*. Accessed 12 December 2021. https://www.brightblue.org.uk/portfolio/home-truths-options-for-reforming/.

Cheshire, P., and Sheppard, S. 1998. 'Estimating the demand for housing, land, and neighbourhood characteristics', *Oxford Bulletin of Economics and Statistics* 60 (3): 357–82.

Corlett, A., and Leslie, J. 2021. 'Home county: Options for taxing main residence capital gains', *Resolution Foundation*. Accessed 12 December 2021. https://www.resolutionfoundation.org/publications/home-county/.

Duca, J. V. 2020. 'Making sense of increased synchronization in global house prices', *Journal of European Real Estate Research* 13 (1): 5–16. https://doi.org/10.1108/JERER-11-2019-0044.

Financial Conduct Authority (FCA). 2021. 'Financial lives 2020 survey: The impact of coronavirus'. Accessed 12 December 2021. https://www.fca.org.uk/publications/research/financial-lives-2020-survey-impact-coronavirus.

Gallent, N., Durrant, D., and May, N. 2017. 'Housing supply, investment demand and money creation: A comment on the drivers of London's housing crisis', *Urban Studies* 54 (10): 2204–16.

Jordà, Ò., Knoll, K., Kuvshinov, D., Schularick, M., and Taylor, A. M. 2019. 'The rate of return on everything, 1870–2015', *Quarterly Journal of Economics* 134 (3): 1225–98.

Kelly, R., McCann, F., and O'Toole, C. 2018. 'Credit conditions, macroprudential policy and house prices', *Journal of Housing Economics* 41: 153–67.

Kohl, S. 2018. 'More mortgages, more homes? The effect of housing financialization on homeownership in historical perspective', *Politics & Society* 46 (2): 177–203.

Leyshon, A., and French, S. 2009. '"We all live in a Robbie Fowler house": The geographies of the buy to let market in the UK', *British Journal of Politics and International Relations* 11 (3): 438–60.

Lyons, M. 2014. *The Lyons Housing Review: Mobilising across the nation to build the homes our children need*. Labour Party. Accessed 24 January 2022. https://www.policyforum.labour.org.uk/uploads/editor/files/The_Lyons_Housing_Review_2.pdf.

Mazzucato, M., and Macfarlane, L. 2017. 'Patient strategic finance: Opportunities for state investment banks in the UK' (UCL Institute for Innovation and Public Purpose Working Paper 2017-05).

Miles, D., and Monro, V. 2019. 'UK house prices and three decades of decline in the risk-free real interest rate' (Bank of England Staff Working Paper No. 837).

Ministry of Housing, Communities and Local Government (MHCLG). 2018. 'Analysis of the determinants of house price changes'. *GOV.UK*. Accessed 12 December 2021. https://www.gov.uk/government/publications/analysis-of-the-determinants-of-house-price-changes.

Ministry of Housing, Communities and Local Government (MHCLG). 2020. 'Planning for the future'. *GOV.UK*. Accessed 12 August 2020. https://www.gov.uk/government/publications/planning-for-the-future.

Ministry of Housing, Communities and Local Government (MHCLG). 2021a. 'Live tables on dwelling stock (including vacants)'. *GOV.UK*. Accessed 12 December 2021. https://www.gov.uk/government/statistical-data-sets/live-tables-on-dwelling-stock-including-vacants.

Ministry of Housing, Communities and Local Government (MHCLG). 2021b. 'Planning applications in England: April to June 2021'. *GOV.UK*. Accessed 12 December 2021. https://www.gov.uk/government/statistics/planning-applications-in-england-april-to-june-2021.

MoneyWeek. 2021. 'Inflation is coming, says the Bank of England – but don't expect us to react'. *MoneyWeek*. Accessed 12 December 2021. https://moneyweek.com/economy/inflation/603465/inflation-is-coming-says-the-bank-of-england.

Moody's Analytics. 2015. 'QE could fuel housing bubbles in Europe'. Accessed 15 December 2018. https://www.economy.com/dismal/analysis/free/255221/QE-Could-Fuel-Housing-Bubbles-in-Europe.

Mulheirn, I. 2019. *Tackling the UK Housing Crisis: Is supply the answer?* UK Collaborative Centre for Housing Evidence report. Accessed 24 January 2022. https://housingevidence.ac.uk/wp-content/uploads/2019/08/20190820-CaCHE-Housing-Supply-FINAL.pdf.

Office for National Statistics (ONS). 2021a. 'Households by household size, regions of England and UK constituent countries'. Accessed 12 December 2021. https://www.ons.gov.uk/peoplepopulationandcommunity/birthsdeathsandmarriages/families/datasets/householdsbyhouseholdsizeregionsofenglandandukconstituentcountries.

Office for National Statistics (ONS). 2021b. 'UK House Price Index: September 2021'. Accessed 11 December 2021. https://www.ons.gov.uk/economy/inflationandpriceindices/bulletins/housepriceindex/september2021.

Partridge, J. 2021. '"Race for space" fuels 10.9% surge in UK house prices', *Guardian*. 1 June 2021. Accessed 26 November 2021. https://www.theguardian.com/money/2021/jun/01/race-for-space-fuels-surge-in-uk-property-prices.

Resolution Foundation. 2020. *Rainy Days*. Resolution Foundation report. Accessed 12 December 2021. https://www.resolutionfoundation.org/publications/rainy-days/.

Ryan-Collins, J. 2018. *Why Can't You Afford a Home?* London: Polity.

Ryan-Collins, J. 2020. 'Boris Johnson's 95% mortgages will put Britain back on course for a house price crash', *Guardian*. 8 October 2020. Accessed 27 March 2021. http://www.theguardian.com/commentisfree/2020/oct/08/boris-johnson-95-per-cent-mortgages-house-price-crash-banking-crisis.

Ryan-Collins, J. 2021a. 'Breaking the housing–finance cycle: Macroeconomic policy reforms for more affordable homes', *Environment and Planning A: Economy and Space* 53 (3): 480–502.

Ryan-Collins, J. 2021b. 'Is the UK housing bubble about to burst? These are the best and worst scenarios', *Guardian*. 2 July 2021. Accessed 12 December 2021. https://www.theguardian.com/commentisfree/2021/jul/02/housing-bubble-birst-uk-gdp-house-prices-interest-rates-economy.

Ryan-Collins, J., Lloyd, T., and Macfarlane, L. 2017. *Rethinking the Economics of Land and Housing*. London: Zed Books.

Schwartz, H., and Seabrooke, L. 2008. 'Varieties of residential capitalism in the international political economy: Old welfare states and the new politics of housing', *Comparative European Politics* 6 (3): 237–61.

The Economist. 2021. 'House prices in the rich world are booming'. 8 April 2021. Accessed 24 January 2022. https://www.economist.com/finance-and-economics/2021/04/08/house-prices-in-the-rich-world-are-booming.

United Nations Human Rights Council (UN HCR). 2017. *Report of the Special Rapporteur on adequate housing as a component of the right to an adequate standard of living. Main focus: Financialization of housing*. New York: United Nations Human Rights Council. https://www.ohchr.org/EN/Issues/Housing/Pages/HousingIndex.aspx.

Part 3
Retaking the economy

8

Bank Job: debt, art, activism and community power

Hilary Powell and Daniel Edelstyn

A chilly Sunday morning in May 2019. A golden Ford Transit van explodes in the shadow of Canary Wharf in London's Docklands. Papers flutter through the morning air, representing the cancellation of £1.2 million of high-interest debt.

This explosion was the dramatic culmination of a journey during which we created our own bank, printed money, issued bonds and built a movement for change. Our artistic/community/activist initiative sought to question moral arguments around debt and challenge the injustice at the heart of the UK's current economic system. We documented this journey in the feature-length film *Bank Job*, released in 2021, and in a book of the same name published by Chelsea Green. This chapter provides a summary of this journey and what it taught us about building concrete alternatives to our current economic malaise.

Opening a community bank

In early 2018 we moved into the former Co-Op Bank on Hoe Street in Walthamstow, London, and launched HSCB: Hoe Street Central Bank. We were inspired by critiques of the financial system (Ross 2004; Graeber 2011) and the work of the Strike Debt movement in the United States, which aimed to challenge and cancel debts following the 2008 financial crash. We wanted to stage our own grassroots experiment in changing the rules of finance. This experiment would both take place in, and benefit, our local community.

We got a small grant from the London Borough of Waltham Forest's arts development team and planned to stage a performance of money creation, which was a comment on the process through which real banks create money out of thin air – 'simply by adding new deposit dollars in accounts on their books in exchange for a borrower's IOU' (Friedman, quoted in Doorman 2015, 4). We gave ourselves the power of a central bank and started to make banknotes on site, using traditional print techniques. We sold these notes at face value for pounds sterling. In place of the Queen and other famous figures from British history, our banknotes featured the faces of local causes. Each figure was produced in denominations of 5, 10, 20, 50, 100 and 1000, so no one was allocated a higher value than the others.

The 'Gary' banknote was named after Gary Nash, founder of Eat or Heat food bank. Gary was totally committed to his work at the food bank – to the detriment of his own precarious position. He lost his job because of his commitment to helping families in need while also caring for his elderly parents and dealing with his own health issues. He was angry at a system that has seen a persistent rise in food bank usage across the UK. His team of committed volunteers include people who once had to turn to the food bank themselves.

The 'Saira' note portrays Saira Mir, who, together with her family, set up a kitchen called Pl84U Al-Suffa. Their mission is to provide free hot meals and a friendly environment to the elderly, people in need, the homeless and those who are living in conditions of social, economic and cultural deprivation and isolation.

The 'Steve' features Stephen Barnabis, who founded The SOUL (Support Our Unique Londoners) Project in 2006. Steve was motivated to do this after his cousin tried to break up a fight and was fatally stabbed in the process. Steve's goal was to provide a safe and inspiring space for young people where they could see the horizon and life beyond their current situation.

The 'Tracey' depicts Tracey Griffiths, the headmistress of Barn Croft Primary School, our children's primary school in Walthamstow. After years of government cuts, 66 out of 67 schools in Waltham Forest are still in crisis, with an £18.4 million shortfall across the borough in 2020. For Barn Croft Primary, this meant a shortfall of £124,260 in 2020 (or £624 per pupil).

HSCB was not just raising money for these local community organisations and services. It was also a community bank in the sense that everyone working there came from the local community, and a community began to form around the bank itself. The team that gathered had their own stories of how debt had touched their lives. Alison, for example, had worked as a teacher in one of our local primary schools but was laid off due to the school's debt from the UK government's private finance initiative, or PFI – a way of creating 'public–private partnerships' in which private firms are contracted to complete and manage public projects, using loans from bond markets or private investors. The firms then charge high rates of interest to the public trust that is responsible for the assets that the project creates.

'I've been a primary school teacher for 33 years', she told us. 'Last summer I was made redundant, quite a shock and surprise. The school I was at is a PFI school, so it means that every year quite a large proportion of their budget has to go to the PFI company, and so five teachers like myself . . . were made redundant' (Edelstyn 2018a; see also Powell and Edelstyn 2020). Such debts have proved incredibly controversial, because the interest rates are widely seen as immoral.

In Walthamstow, our health trust, Barts, is the most indebted in the country in terms of PFI (Lister 2015). To pay these debts, the hospitals have to cut staff, and they are therefore overcrowded and dangerously under-resourced. An excellent report from the BBC showed that five of the biggest PFI companies are based in tax havens, despite earning more than £2 billion in profit (Hosken 2017).

Isabell was another member of HSCB – a banknote printer who was also a recent graduate. 'I've spent seven years of my life in education,' she said. 'Coming out of Uni today, young people are just saddled with this huge debt burden. I've got credit cards, personal loans, overdrafts, I've got student loans' (Edelstyn 2018b; see also Powell & Edelstyn 2020).

To run our bank, we borrowed pieces of equipment and drew on the talent of our community in setting up what we needed to design and print the new currency. It became a sort of DIY uprising – a space of work and play, with economics talks laid on in the evenings for anyone who wanted to come and learn.

We initially had doubts about whether anyone would understand what we were up to. A public relations person told us it was all a bit too 'lofty'. We worried that the whole thing might flop. However, as more and more local people began to join us in printing the money, something amazing began to happen. What had started out in our imaginations began to turn into a vehicle which had some form of momentum, rallying against a system that we felt had let us down. Our rebel bank was becoming a place to come together and discover the collective power of art, sharing and community action to defy the alienating power that financial capital has in our lives.

When an article about the bank was published in the *Guardian* (Leach 2018) and went viral, people travelled from all over Britain and queued around the block to buy banknotes. £40,000 was raised through the sale of these notes as artworks. Half of the money we raised was given to the four causes depicted on the notes. The other half of the money was used to buy up £1.2 million worth of local payday loans – very high-interest, short-term lending used mostly by low-income households. These were purchased on secondary debt markets, where lenders can sell on defaulted loans to other collectors at a discount. We discovered you can buy up people's distressed debts for as little as 2 per cent of their original value. It began to feel like we were active agents of change, working with, for and through our community.

How did the project change people who came into contact with it? At one level, having even part of your debts written off through a simple act of citizen intervention felt good. However, this was not a hack that could be used to fix the entire system. Rather, it was a dramatic way of drawing people into the story of debt and exposing not only the mechanisms of the secondary debt markets but also the illegitimacy and hypocrisy of many debts. While crisis-stricken banks benefitted from vast government bailouts and corporate debt is regularly written off, individual borrowers often face aggressive loan enforcement and strong pressure to repay as a moral obligation. Exposing this can enable a different conversation with creditors chasing people for debts that are in some sense imaginary and empower further education and action around an unjust system.

More broadly, it was about democracy. In *Creditocracy: And the case for debt refusal*, Andrew Ross reflects on the expansion of loans for vital aspects of life, like education. Many of these can never be fully repaid and will benefit the 'creditor class' without generating wider prosperity. He argues:

> . . . loading debt onto the citizenry inflicts grievous harm on any democracy . . . When a government cannot – or will not – respond [on behalf of a citizenry], then taking debt relief for ourselves may be the most indispensable act of civil disobedience. Asserting the moral right to repudiate debt may be the only way of rebuilding popular democracy (Ross 2004, 100).

Big Bang 2

After we had sold enough banknotes to fund four local causes and buy up and abolish £1.2 million of high-interest debt, we wanted to bring this subversive act to life with a visceral and visual act. We had been filming everything from the beginning and had decided to make a documentary film in the style of the heist genre. What better climax to a heist than an explosion?

However, in order to do this, we needed more money. Thankfully, when you are a bank, this is not a problem. You just create it yourself. This time we decided to issue bonds, traditionally a way for one entity to raise money by borrowing from another. Bonds are debt-based and deliver a return for investors. In times of conflict, governments issue war bonds, calling on citizens and investors to loan them money in order to fund whatever endeavour they are involved with. Government debt is seen as the safest place for investors to put their money, particularly in volatile times with a fragile financial system. We saw our debt issue as a form of war bond – a cry to join us in exploding the conversation around debt and our current economic system. Our bonds were debt-based but did not yield financial return in the same way as traditional bonds. The return on investment was listed as:

- The bond itself – an artwork printed in the bank using traditional print techniques of letterpress, screen print, foil block and company seal with a finishing touch of gilt (another word for bonds is Gilts or gilt-edged securities).
- An invitation to the explosion.
- A fragment of the explosion: after the explosion, we collected the exploded parts of the van, exhibited them in suspended animation and then melted them down to create commemorative coins – turning debt back into currency and providing a return more valuable than the initial investment.
- The chance to make history.

As people began to buy these in a move to support the endeavour, we worked frantically behind the scenes to make sure this event would actually take place. The production line kicked in and the team got together for this final job. The bank opened its doors once again for more making and debating. To produce another design in place of the faces of Gary, Saira, Steve and Tracey, we borrowed one of our children's toy trucks and, with more difficulty than expected, smashed it up and photographed it in various configurations. With the help of our neighbour graphic designer Phil Seddon, we created versions of an exploded image. These were pressed onto the bonds alongside the words 'This bond is issued by Hoe Street Central Bank. The holder of this bond is entitled to a fragment of the remains of the collectively owned and distributed explosion of £1 million of payday debt – Big Bang 2.'

Why did we call our explosion Big Bang 2? Because we wanted to make the symbolic destruction of debt visceral and real. The explosion and the sculpture we subsequently created from the fragments were designed to shake the foundations of both capital and art, by provoking questioning of our current debt-fuelled economic system. There is a trajectory of banking deregulation and a financialisation of society over the last 30 to 40 years that owes its origins to something that began happening in our childhoods and which forged a path to the bailout of the too-big-to-fail banks in 2008 and the personal debt crisis happening in its wake: Big Bang 1.

On 27 October 1986, as part of the privatisation led by UK Prime Minister Margaret Thatcher's Conservative government, the London Stock Exchange became a private limited company. The City – London's finance centre – was in effect deregulated. Changes in the structure of financial markets and trading culture included the removal of fixed commission charges and the switch to electronic trading. These changes, which became known as the Big Bang, made London a major player on the international finance stage. The Big Bang was an explosion of speculation and the beginning of investment banking, hedge funds and bonus culture in the UK. It was a period of massive acquisitions and mergers. Power was concentrated as big companies took over many other smaller, long-standing City firms. It was the beginning of too-big-to-fail corporations dominating financial centres and making them increasingly fragile. Meanwhile, in the US, the Glass–Steagall Act still separated risky investment banking from deposit taking, so American firms crowded into the newly deregulated space created in London.

The impacts were far reaching – from changing high-street banking to slowly eroding the structure of society. Big Bang was a defining moment in which the latent power of finance, which had been regulated to serve the needs of the people, was set free. Big Bang was the moment when those in charge of the City rapidly became 'Masters of the Universe' (as Tom Wolfe dubbed investment bankers and traders in his 1987 satire, *The Bonfire of the Vanities*). So little is publicly understood about this paradigm shift away from the social contract, and yet it has shaped our moral universe and personal narratives.

Thatcher understood the power of language. Her agenda was promoted with the buzzwords 'freedom', 'choice', 'opportunity' and 'prosperity'. These were hard to argue with, resonating with some of humankind's most deeply rooted psychological desires. These words promoted Thatcher's drive towards the all-encompassing privatisation of public services: 'Nothing less than a crusade to enfranchise the many in the economy of the nation. We, the Conservatives, are returning power to the people' (Thatcher 1986). Offering shares in formerly public companies promised a different form of democratic public ownership. But dream and reality ruptured. This mass privatisation has led to dysfunction and exploitation – with public services monopolised by overseas firms and investment groups able to make huge profits by exploiting a captive market.

Perhaps Thatcher's most infamous phrase was 'there is no alternative' (TINA). TINA became a rallying cry for neoliberalism – free markets, free trade, free enterprise. The key word is 'free'. But this freedom seems only to apply to one tier of society. There is freedom for the few – freedom to take profits offshore, to indebt the public services through PFI, freedom to privatise our public goods – and debt peonage for the rest. Free education and a health-care system that is free at the point of access – these freedoms have been continuously eroded, forcing many to turn to welfare or debt in order to survive. These people are then labelled scroungers in an ongoing rhetoric against the poor and vulnerable. TINA returned with a vengeance in a speech by Conservative Prime Minister David Cameron in 2013: 'If there was another way, I would take it. But there is no alternative' (Robinson 2013). Cameron used these words to defend massive cuts in spending that would characterise the decade of austerity that the UK and other countries experienced following the 2008 financial crash. Austerity policies have further eroded and diminished public services. In societal terms, this is an idea of freedom gone awry – freedom divorced from responsibility and accountability. *Liberté* without the *Egalité* and *Fraternité*.

Entering the stronghold

Big Bang 2 was staged on a rubble-strewn waste ground jutting out into the Royal Docks next to Millennium Mills and owned by the London Development Authority. This was a site with a clear view towards the ethereal towers of the Docklands. This was the 'money shot' of the money-making project. Our chance to turn the power of this iconic skyline against itself with an iconoclastic act.

In his opus *Passagenwerk* (The Arcades Project), Walter Benjamin (1999) argues that we need to re-appropriate these city images and spaces to create layered personal records of travels and explorations that can puncture these scenographic compositions of place and transform these spectacles of might. Big Bang 2 sought to create a form of ethical, emancipatory spectacle (Boyd and Duncombe 2004; Duncombe 2007) to puncture the spectacular image. The towers of Canary Wharf embody what situationist Debord (1970, 34) understands and explores in *The Society of the Spectacle*: 'The spectacle is capital to such a degree of accumulation that it becomes an image.' In this part of London, capital has accumulated fast through the erasure of various pasts. The iconic Docklands skyline has become an image and spectacle to overrule memory and dissent.

And aside from all that, every good heist needs an explosion. This was to be our 'You're only supposed to blow the bloody doors off' moment.

The decisive moment

Blowing up an empty van on an empty lot in a now-deserted part of East London threw up more challenges than we initially anticipated. We had to wade into a Kafkaesque labyrinth of bureaucratic procedures and rules. There would be no children, no press, no more people, no broadcasting of the time and place of this event to anyone beyond the invited bondholders. However, on the day the prison of rules receded. Outside the danger zone of the explosion itself there was a jaunty, relaxed air. People strolled onto the site chatting and sharing in the rapidly dwindling supply of morning coffee and croissants. The weather was misty – an act of God intervening on behalf of big capital – but as we prepped and positioned cameras, the clouds lifted just enough to make a viable shot. Our golden van was rolled into its designated spot. The 'bomb' – a water bomb developed for use in anti-terror operations where the speed of the water is faster than the electrical discharge of the device – was placed and primed. The explosives team set down the debts – stacks of hand-stamped paper notes stating 'this note represents £200 of £1.2 million of exploded debt' – and we made our way outside of the frag zone.

3   2   1   and   FIRING!

The slow-motion camera operator said he had never been so anxious at a shoot. There was no leeway for the 8 seconds of footage that this advanced 'Phantom' could capture. It was a gathering and a gift. We were shocked that some people travelled miles to share in the moment and bear witness. In the wreckage of Big Bang 2, some were weeping. As the *New York Times* photographer took our photographs, clad in grey overalls and security helmets with HSCB branding, we felt relief and exhaustion. No one had been hurt, and no one had stopped us. We had gotten away with it. Up to a point. The pressures exerted on us had succeeded in ensuring this was not the press spectacle we had hoped for. It did not pierce the public narrative as intended. However, the explosion was 'in the can', with more opportunities to continue its dissemination in our film.

After the explosion, the audience surrounded the skeletal remains of the van in an ad hoc ritual circle, taking multiple pictures and picking up the scattered papers. We were enveloped in a strange and cathartic peace. As we stayed on site, mapping and clearing up the minutiae of the aftermath of the explosion, the first planes of the day began flying overhead, taking off from the adjacent City Airport with deafening force. It was business as usual after our short, anarchic interlude.

Ironically, the doors were the only thing that hadn't blown off.

Knowledge is power

Central to our Bank Job is the idea that knowledge is power. This knowledge is learned and communicated in many forms. For us, the idea of thinking through making is central – making visible, tactile and malleable the forces that we are told to believe are immutable. We believe in an empowered knowledge through participation and action. The Bank Job has been an exercise in creative destruction. We sought to question and shatter outmoded ways of thinking, to construct new strategies and tactics of being.

There is a sense that, as artists, we are not qualified or allowed to speak in this arena. On the one hand, there is an increasing dismissal of experts, and on the other, a denigration and marginalisation of voices that speak truth to power. Yet, here we are, engaging and acting, aware of both our limitations and our potent strength. We are obliged to educate ourselves. We have a responsibility to share knowledge and a commitment to using the tools we have – our imagination and making, both physically and digitally. Those that can move beyond conventional political circles are harder to categorise and therefore harder to repress and control. Artists are committed doers and organisers – resourceful visionaries well placed to imagine and implement a better world.

Debt and freedom

To talk about debt is to talk about freedom. Debt, democracy and the imagination are inextricably bound. People declare themselves 'debt free' as a mark of honour and often in a way that dismisses those living in the debt trap. In reality, from nation states to individuals, none of us are debt free. Even if not personally in debt (and those people are fewer than you think, considering mortgages, credit cards, student loans, overdrafts, etc.), we are all collectively indebted through an unjust economic system.

Contrary to a blind faith in a benevolent establishment, we believe 'power concedes nothing without a demand. It never did and it never will' (Douglass 1957). Above all, this project has been an act of liberation – freeing ourselves and hopefully others from the limited imagination and language surrounding debt. Freeing us from playing the rules of a game managed in the name of the 1 per cent. Freeing us from a system where the house always wins.

The psychological impacts of being in debt are well known. Lifting the humiliation and stigma of debt is critical. However, there is also a wider psychology to tackle. We need to move beyond sympathy, even empathy, for poor people in debt, to recognise that we do indeed live in a creditocracy – where the finance sector exerts excessive influence over governments while we citizens depend on debt to meet our basic needs (Ross 2004). Such recognition enables us to change a system that relies on both our private, individualised shame and our collective consent.

At the centre of our Bank Job has been the acquisition and cancellation of £1.2 million of predatory personal debt by intervening in the secondary debt markets. The point of this act was not charitable. We did not focus on the difference this might make to those individuals whose debt was written off. We did not want to foreground specific debtors, who might be either blamed or pitied. Instead, our highly visible, symbolic act was designed to be a rallying cry and lightning rod for collective solidarity and public education. It was designed to kickstart a campaign for a large-scale personal debt write-off across the UK, by making the case for how this would benefit us all.

From Bank Job to power

Bank Job has taught us that people are hungry for change. They are tired of the status quo. They want to participate in projects that seek to transform and redefine what it is to be a human being in the twenty-first century.

We also learned that we all have to live our purpose. To take on the world of capital and the spectre of debt demands huge commitment and collective action. Now we are embarking on our new project, which examines and attempts to intervene in the world of finance and the climate catastrophe. Focused on energy democracy and an idea of infrastructure as resistance, we are building a co-operatively owned energy company that attempts to get our street and then many more as close to off-grid as possible through enacting a grassroots green new deal. None of this would have been possible without a rebellious spark in our imaginations which began to grow when it came into contact with others. All these projects are like seeds in the wind, travelling to fertile ground in other places and at other times. In order to build a truly prosperous and fair society, we must start by allowing our imaginations to be free. As Lucy Lippard (1984) states, 'the power of art is subversive rather than authoritarian, lying in its ability to see – and then in its power to make others see that they too can make something of what they see . . . and so on.'

References

Benjamin, W. 1999. *The Arcades Project*. Cambridge, MA: Harvard University Press.
Boyd, A., and Duncombe, S. 2004. 'The manufacture of dissent: What the Left can learn from Las Vegas', *Journal of Aesthetics and Protest* 1 (3): n.p. Accessed 2 August 2021. http://www.joaap.org/new3/duncombeboyd.html.
Debord, G. 1970. *The Society of the Spectacle*. Detroit: Black and Red.
Doorman, F. 2015. *Our Money: Towards a new monetary system*. London: Positive Money. Accessed 2 August 2021. https://positivemoney.org/wp-content/uploads/2015/10/Our-Money-06-4-2015-A5-Download-Positive-Money-28-8-2015-2.pdf.
Douglass, F. 1957. 'West India emancipation' speech delivered at Canandaigua, New York, 3 August 1857. University of Rochester Frederick Douglass Project. Accessed 2 August 2021. https://rbscp.lib.rochester.edu/4398.
Duncombe, S. 2007. *Dream: Re-imagining progressive politics in an age of fantasy*. New York: The New Press.
Edelstyn, D. 2018a. 'Meet Alison'. Accessed 2 August 2021. https://vimeo.com/271975525.
Edelstyn, D. 2018b. 'Meet Isobell'. Accessed 2 August 2021. https://vimeo.com/271975975.
Graeber, D. 2011. *Debt: The first five thousand years*. London: Melville House.
Hosken, A. 2017. 'PFI: Five firms avoid tax despite £2bn profits, BBC learns', *BBC News*. 27 October 2017. Accessed 2 August 2021. https://www.bbc.co.uk/news/business-41778609.
Leach, A. 2018. 'The rebel bank, printing its own notes and buying back people's debts', *Guardian*. 21 March 2021. Accessed 2 August 2021. https://www.theguardian.com/world/2018/mar/23/hoe-street-central-bank-walthamstow-london-debt.

Lippard, L. 1984. 'Trojan horses: Activist art and power'. In *Art After Modernism: Rethinking representation*, ed. Brian Wallis, 341–58. Boston: David R. Godine.

Lister, J. 2015. 'Bart's: A flagship hits the rocks of PFI', *Open Democracy*. 18 March 2015. Accessed 2 August 2021. https://www.opendemocracy.net/en/ournhs/barts-flagship-hits-rocks-of-pfi/.

Powell, H., and Edelstyn, D. 2020. *Bank Job*. London: Chelsea Green Publishing.

Robinson, N. 2013. 'Economy: There is no alternative (TINA) is back', *BBC News*. 7 March 2013. Accessed 2 August 2021. https://www.bbc.co.uk/news/uk-politics-21703018.

Ross, A. 2004. *Creditocracy: And the case for debt refusal*. New York City: OR Books.

Thatcher, M. 1986. 'Speech to Conservative Party Conference', 10 October 1986. *Margaret Thatcher Foundation*. Accessed 2 August 2021. https://www.margaretthatcher.org/document/106498.

9

Money Advice and Education: creating community endurance and prosperity

Christopher Harker and Jerry During[1]

Private debts are relations between a creditor (for example a bank or local council) and a debtor (almost always an individual). However, while the debtor is legally responsible as an individual for repaying their debt, the actual lived experience of repaying and struggling with debts often extends well beyond that person, affecting and impacting their family, friends, colleagues and other people in their social network as they ask for support or relationships deteriorate. Most current practices in the UK for supporting struggling debtors focus on the indebted individual. However, this chapter argues for forms of intervention that work with the broader community in which debtors are enfolded. This argument learns from the work of Money Advice and Education (Money A+E), a social enterprise based in East London. Money A+E provides money advice and educational services to what it terms Diverse Ethnic Communities (DECs); this nomenclature avoids the use of colour or continents to describe people and the risks of inaccurate labelling and stereotyping connected with such practices.[2] Money A+E currently provides six services, including two mentorship programmes at an NVQ level that train school pupils and community volunteers to become financial mentors, financial confidence workshops that teach financial knowledge and skills, a regular newsletter, a money champions scheme that trains volunteers and staff working in community-facing organisations to give a basic money guidance session and a money coaching service providing social welfare law advice for those with personal debt and benefit problems. Since the outbreak of the Covid-19 pandemic, these services have been offered remotely through digital platforms and by phone, as well as some outreach sessions in person.

These practices are innovative because they largely focus on the way debtors are part of broader social networks and they resist the various processes through which indebtedness induces people to behave as isolated individuals. They foreground community-led solutions to problems of debt. To outline how this happens, this chapter begins by contextualising Money A+E's interventions in relation to the UK's debt crisis and its impact on advice services. The growing and intractable problem of the deficit budget, where a debtor's outgoing repayments exceed their income, means that no amount of education, financial planning or debt restructuring can ultimately solve the problems many debtors in the UK currently face. Broader solutions are needed that combat poverty and increasing costs of living by addressing high housing costs and low-paying work, as well as cancelling debt.

While waiting for such systems to be put in place, Money A+E and similar organisations seek to capacitate marginalised communities to find alternative options that enable them to overcome problem debt and financial hardship. The second part of the chapter therefore describes Money A+E's work in detail. A case study of a mentoring programme in North London is used to illustrate both the problems debt is causing and the innovative ways in which Money A+E's work tries to address such challenges. The third part of the chapter reflects on the lived experiences of debt that form the basis for Money A+E's interventions. Debtors are often isolated from their friends and family while simultaneously drawing on their social connections and relationships to endure the debilitating conditions of problem debt. Working at the intersection of the individual and their broader social network demands consideration of the social inequalities that striate British society. Many of the current problems of debt are experienced unequally not just according to socio-economic group but also according to ethnicity. In the UK, 'Asian and Black households and those in the Other ethnic group were more likely to be poor and were the most likely to be in persistent poverty' (UK Government Cabinet Office 2018, 9). In conclusion, we argue that Money A+E's work not only enables communities to endure, but also actively contributes to building and sustaining forms of prosperity that are particularly salient to the marginalised communities with which they work.

Indebtedness within the UK and its impact on advice services

In the UK, levels of personal debt reached an all-time high even before the Covid-19 outbreak (see Harker, chapter 1). Consequently, debt-related problems have proliferated. Over eight million people were facing crisis debt in 2018, with up to 60 per cent of people in England and Wales seeking debt advice and support unable to access it, a figure which was as high as 80 per cent in London (Money Advice Service 2018, 3). Since the Covid-19 pandemic began, the number of people seeking advice has grown. For instance, in 2019, Money A+E supported 314 people with its debt advice service. In 2020, it supported 670 with the same service, an 112 per cent increase in clients. Recent initiatives to support debtors will also increase demand for advice services. For instance, new breathing-space legislation (officially called the Debt Respite Scheme) grants debtors a 60-day period during which they are protected from enforcement action by creditors and interest, fees and charges are frozen. Those seeking this two-month repayment hiatus have to seek debt advice or treatment in instances of mental health crisis (Jones 2019).

The nature of problem debt has also shifted from excessive consumer spending to priority debts such as rent arrears, council tax arrears and fuel debts (Kirwan 2019a). Debts are now being taken on because families can no longer afford to pay for basic necessities. Table 9.1 illustrates the increasing proportion of Money A+E service users that face priority debt repayments.

Such problems have been caused by austerity politics that have reduced state-based social support systems in multiple ways. Over half (54 per cent) of those in problem debt in the UK receive support through the social security system (StepChange 2020, 2). The most emblematic and

Table 9.1 Percentage of Money A+E service users experiencing priority debts, 2019–21.

	2019	2020	2021*
Total number of cases	232	670	573
Rent & mortgage arrears	1%	16%	30%
Council tax arrears	1%	10%	16%
Utility debts	4%	12%	26%

*As of 25 April 2021.

significant cause of hardship has been the introduction of Universal Credit (UC). Those most in need of income support have to survive for periods of up to six weeks without any benefit payments as they are transitioned to the UC system. Among those affected by the wait for UC, 60 per cent ask for financial help from family or friends (StepChange 2020, 9).

Once in the system, 'overpayments' of benefits (often due to provider-side errors) have been clawed back by reducing future benefit payments. This often causes households' existing financial crises to cascade out of control, as reduced incomes cannot repay previous debts, and thus forces people to take out further loans. Advice organisations report that over 95 per cent of rent arrears were caused by UC (StepChange 2020, 68). This context is crucial for understanding the problem of households' deficit budgets, where incomes are so low that there is no way to cover all necessary outgoings, in some cases even without debt repayments factored in. Debt advice and support services are left trying to solve a financial crisis through a budget sheet that will not, and cannot, add up. In a 2020 survey of StepChange clients, only 6 per cent of respondents reported they were able to make ends meet every month, while 46 per cent reported that they never did (StepChange 2020, 3).

Another austerity-induced change that has impacted Money A+E's work is the sharp contraction of the advice sector after massive reductions in legal aid and council funding (T. Barrett 2019, 67). Like many other public service providers, advice agencies are now severely overstretched. This manifests in a reduced capacity to support vulnerable debtors seeking support. The increasing digitisation of benefits and other services means people struggling from problem debts are more reliant than ever on third parties like Money A+E to help them with applications and challenging decisions. Digitisation often increases the time that it takes advice providers to deal with benefit problems, because they are no longer able to speak with an official agent on the phone. These pressures further increase the need for skills sharing within communities and can be understood as the state deliberately relying on the shadow state to provide basic services at the same time as it is reducing funding for such services.

Money A+E: capacitating community endurance

Money A+E was founded in 2011 by Jerry During, Greg Ashby and Farah Ashraf. On the Money A+E website, Jerry describes growing up in a family experiencing severe financial issues. He cites personal relationships and expert advice as the two key factors that enabled his family to endure their financial challenges. Greg also describes the important role these factors played in helping him face the threat of small-business bankruptcy. It is precisely these lived experiences of personal financial crisis that led Greg and his co-founders to create a money advice and education service that focused on the community rather than individuals.

When this chapter was completed (June 2021), Money A+E had 14 members of staff, and utilised hundreds of hours of volunteer support. In 2020, it supported 522 advice cases and helped over 1,000 adults and young people through its mentoring programmes. While deeply rooted in Newham, Money A+E now works across 10 London boroughs. There are efforts to scale this work through the Inclusive Economy Partnership (IEP), which is a partnership of businesses, civil society and government departments that are working together to help communities feel they belong to and can participate in the UK economy. The partnership has a wide variety of public, private and third-sector agencies which cannot all be mentioned here. As a steering committee member and social innovation partner on the accelerator programme, Money A+E worked closely with the following partners: the Cabinet Office, the Office for Civil Society, The Young Foundation, Nesta, Fair4All Finance, the Money and Pensions Service, Nationwide Building Society and many more. Such partnerships allow sharing of knowledge and coordination of practices.

Money A+E is also seeking to expand with regard to the provision of integrated services, through a Social Housing Learning and Support Centre (SHLSC). Housing and homelessness have been central to many of the debt issues Money A+E service users face, particularly since the onset of the Covid-19 pandemic (Harker, Huq and Charalambous 2020). The SHLSC is intended to provide temporary affordable accommodation to young homeless single people and young single people leaving care, combined with wrap-around well-being, employability and financial education support and training.

The key to Money A+E's approach is not just helping individuals solve their immediate financial problems – although this is an important step; it is also ensuring that this process builds greater capacity and knowledge at the community level. It is useful to examine one of the services Money A+E provides – the money mentors course – to get a detailed understanding of how this is put into practice. The course teaches essential skills and knowledge about personal finance, helping people to manage their money and feel increasingly confident in doing so. The course is often promoted with the headline that participants can gain £500 through employing the skills taught to maximise incomes and minimise expenses. However, the course also embeds skills and knowledge that can be shared with participants' families and communities. The course is Ofqual-recognised at Level 2 (equivalent to a GCSE grade of 4–9 or an NVQ Level 1), so completing it gives participants a formal qualification and transferable skills for employability. Hence, the course can be part of a broader programme of educational attainment and life-building skills. Once they complete the course, older participants not in education are recruited to continue volunteering as money mentors and, where possible, employed as apprentice training co-ordinators and money coach advisers to expand Money A+E's reach into the communities in which they work. Working in this way means the mentoring programme creates an ever-expanding community of knowledge and action. Training service users to become service providers also means that those delivering the training understand the money challenges faced by those seeking support. This is crucial for embedding empathy and understanding in the advice process, which, in turn, is essential when working with people whose financial difficulties make them feel judged, punished and ashamed. Increasing the number of people who can support others with debt advice is a way of breaking down the taboos that often surround money matters in communities and families. Mentoring also seeks to ease the pressure on the team of money coaches who deliver one-to-one advice, crucial in a context where service providers are overworked and underfunded.

Money A+E's method – targeting debt problems via the community rather than at an individual level – can be seen clearly in a 2019 mentorship programme in Enfield. Money A+E's schools mentoring programme usually works with 16–18-year-old youth who attend schools and colleges. As with the community mentoring scheme, the goal is to teach essential life skills with regard to successfully managing money. However, a schools' trust in Enfield invited Money A+E to run a programme in a primary school. Instead of working with pupils, the participants were parents. School teachers and administrators were motivated to hire Money A+E because they were seeing the effects of poverty and high levels of debt at the school gates and in the classrooms. Young children would arrive at school without being properly fed but would already know what a bailiff was. Prior to contacting Money A+E, the school was already providing a food bank once a week to support low-income parents. The mentoring programme in this school provided financial education to parents who were struggling with rent arrears, energy debts and council tax debts. The aim was for those parents in turn to share the skills and knowledge gained from the programme with their families and other pupils' parents. Of the 17 people who undertook the mentoring course, 12 completed it, receiving qualifications equivalent to a good GCSE. Participants reported measurable increases in confidence and well-being. In her feedback to Money A+E, Dorothy, a parent who had participated in the course, focused on the skills she had gained. She reported creating a household budget for her family, which they have stuck to, and checking bank statements. Feedback from Sonia, another parent participant, focused on the value of addressing debt collectively. 'You got to hear other people's stories and it sort of helps you to evaluate your own situation . . . It's just about connecting people, hearing their stories and I found it quite empowering actually.' Karen, a parent support officer working at the school, also noted forms of communal practice that had developed through the course itself: 'Parents themselves have seemed to have opened up and built a sort of friendship amongst themselves to support each other.' These examples show the modest but meaningful ways in which Money A+E's advice has enabled one school-based community to address debt problems. Skills such as budgeting and communal support networks help people manage money and related issues both practically and emotionally. From 2018 to 2022 Money A+E dealt with more than 1600 people, helping them manage over £6 million worth of debt and maximising their income by £1.5 million. More broadly, four out of every five Money A+E service users report a positive experience, and three-quarters of service users can identify, set and achieve money goals and feel in control of how they budget, spend and manage money (Harker and Anderson 2020, 6).

Isolated individuals

One of the most significant problems advice services face is that practices of taking out a loan and then experiencing indebtedness can be highly individualising and isolating. Prior to the Covid-19 pandemic, one in four Money A+E service users reported that they did not feel included in society overall (Harker and Anderson 2020, 7). The pandemic has increased social isolation and reduced access to social networks and support (Harker, Huq and Charalambous 2020), resulting in a 'second pandemic', this time in mental health (Mind 2020). When people enter into a debt relation with an institution such as a bank or high-cost credit provider, a legally binding contract formalises or embodies the debt relation. In most cases, a named individual becomes solely liable for that debt. If borrowers miss payments or default, creditors employ a range of techniques to target them, mixing letter writing, telephone calls and text messages (Deville 2015). Such practices cause anxiety and stress that can isolate debtors from their family and friends. The speed and repetition of creditor communications, and the messages contained within them, also actively seek to disconnect debtors from other debts they owe in order to prioritise repayment of the creditor's loan.

The effects of isolation and the impact of debt on mental and physical well-being and healthy social relations is well documented (Mind 2011; Deville 2015; Davey 2019; Money and Mental Health 2019). Davies, Montgomerie and Wallin (2015) use the term 'financial melancholia' to describe the mental and physical illnesses resulting from problem debts that people struggle to or cannot repay. This in turn feeds into emotional turmoil, chronic stress and anxiety at the household level, which may further isolate individuals from their family or those closest to them. 'Individual efforts to take complete responsibility for [debt] lead to manic, unrealistic dreams of escape (sometimes manifesting in further spending), whereas successful strategies involve seeking help and sympathy from others. Individualised perspectives on debt are part of the problem, not the solution' (Davies, Montgomerie and Wallin 2015, 5). Dawney (2019, 50) notes that even when people are not experiencing debt as a problem, 'the pressure of being in debt is felt in low-level ways and in ways we aren't always aware of', leading to 'a generalised sense of being overwhelmed or of juggling too much'. This creates a state of hypervigilance – 'a mild fear of impending danger' – and a 'background of anxiety' that wears people down. In a 2020 survey of Money A+E service users, respondents recorded significantly lower levels of satisfaction, happiness and a sense that life is worthwhile, along with higher levels of anxiety, than the national average (Harker and Anderson 2020, 7).

The morality of debt repayment plays a key role in such processes, further isolating debtors. Being indebted is often considered shameful, which means many debtors keep their problems secret from those around them. One in five Money A+E service users reported not seeking help with money issues for over a year (Harker and Anderson 2020, 5). As an article about PayPlan, a telephone helpline providing one of the UK's largest debt advice services, noted, 'Most people have been struggling on for months, if not years. Most have kept their debt problems a secret, and the stress is taking a toll on their mental health . . . Problem debt is usually a private battle' (C. Barrett 2019, n.p.). In other contexts, it is worth noting how the widely held belief that it is morally good to repay one's debts has been used in forms of micro-finance. Across the Global South, micro-finance organisations provide small amounts of credit to groups of borrowers who have no traditional financial resources. Loans are secured through peer liability, where debt is given to a group of kin or an existing social network. All members of the group are equally liable for repayments. This process draws its power from the morality, shame and exclusion that operates within peer groups if one member does not repay (Karim 2008).

In the UK, some aspects of the debt advice process unintentionally reinforce the individual nature of debt. Debtors, whether in person or on the phone, are almost always consulted one-to-one, as this is crucial for maintaining confidentiality. Part of the advice process – described in detail by Kirwan (2019a, 321) – focuses on mapping relationships between the debtor and their creditors, 'establishing the specific powers, procedures and actors associated with each debt'. After conducting research on advice agencies in the UK, James (2019, 88) reflects, 'I often thought that the organisation of the welfare system and the debt advice sector might have been organised in a less individualised way. Rather than making people feel alone in their suffering, there could have been more emphasis on community and relationships.' Kirwan (2019a, 321) notes that debt advisers will map out the relationships between 'the debtor and their significant others, assigning relevant flows of liability and financial responsibility as well as further bonds of "informal" debt and credit'. However, the process itself remains individualised.

Social networks as support systems

Experiences of debt are bifurcated. Debtors are isolated as individuals in the ways described above. However, they often simultaneously draw on financial, social and emotional resources provided by family, friends and colleagues to endure their conditions of indebtedness. For example, users of the debt advice line PayPlan include a woman who used her son's phone because she could not afford her own mobile. Another is not a debtor herself, but a guarantor who phoned because her brother missed repayments on a loan, for which she was now liable (C. Barrett 2019). This reflects the practices of lenders such as Amigo, a high-cost credit provider which provides guarantor loans – a form of credit that targets the ways in which debtors rely on friend and family relationships to both borrow and repay loans (Makortoff 2019). In May 2021, Amigo was banned from making further loans by the Financial Conduct Authority because it had mis-sold products, following claims by the families and friends of debtors that they had not agreed to become guarantors or had been pressurised into doing so (Jones 2021; Sweney 2021). Social relationships are folded into debt relations in other ways, as families create budgets and reduce expenses to enable debt repayments and perform emotional labour to support the member responsible for debt repayment (Harker, Sayyad and Shebeitah 2019).

While credit providers like Amigo are exploiting the more-than-individual experience of indebtedness, there are emerging forms of practice which take the sociality of debt as the starting point for practices of dealing with and resisting debt. Stanley, Deville and Montgomerie (2016) explore the collective forms of response that are created through debt-specific subforums and threads on the peer-to-peer information exchange websites Consumer Action Group, Money Saving Expert and Mumsnet. Such sites provide an alternative to conventional sources of debt advice, drawing legitimacy from everyday experiences of living with/in debt. Site participants provide '"Troubleshooting", a form of interaction in which online communities collectively respond and support a debtor with a particular problem; [and] "Journeying", a form of interaction in which online communities collectively coalesce around the emotional, practical and mundane dimensions of a debtor's "journey" towards debt freedom' (Stanley, Deville and Montgomerie 2016, 69). Collectively, such practices 'perform or enact alternative visions of economic relations' (Stanley, Deville and Montgomerie 2016, 78) which focus on practical techniques and emotional support. As the authors note in conclusion, the forums demonstrate that debtors have 'considerable resilience in the face [of] the various challenges that they have to confront' (Stanley, Deville and Montgomerie 2016, 81).

In Spain, the *Platforma de Afectados por la Hipoteca* (PAH, Platform for people affected by mortgages) has become an iconic example of collective debt resistance (Berglund 2019; Gutierrez Garza 2019). Founded in the aftermath of the 2008 financial crisis that left thousands of homeowners unable to pay their mortgages and facing foreclosure, PAH has prevented evictions through direct action, engaged in non-violent protest and created a political platform for promoting change and debtor solidarity (Gutierrez Garza 2019, 27). Such practices might be one example of what Kirwan (2019b, 138) has in mind when he calls for a form of critical financial capability that equips people to 'talk about debt without shame; fend off anxiety about enforcement communally [and] enable each other to write down and write off their debts'. We argue that Money A+E's work can be considered another means of building critical financial capability. Critical here means going beyond practices that enable negotiation of the present financial system to build capacity for alternative ways of financing life. By targeting debtors as members of social networks, workplaces and communities, Money A+E seeks to build relationships that will support individuals suffering from debt. This process puts communal resources – in the form of knowledge and empathy – in place which enable a collective response to debt problems and the broader landscape of austerity-induced inequality and poverty. In such processes, communities themselves are both creators and deliverers of solutions. With a more supportive policy environment, such communal resources could provide the basis of an alternative, more equitable and just economic system. However, it is crucial to recognise that the present landscape is experienced differently because it is shaped by social inequalities.

Debt and ethnicity

While this chapter foregrounds Money A+E's practice as a means through which people can deal with debt problems collectively, it is important to remember that many individuals suffer from debt problems precisely because they lack access to strong social networks. For instance, migrants may be distanced from family and friends in ways that prevent easy and quick access to support in times of emergency. Those living with low or no incomes over long periods may exhaust forms of support from family and friends. Furthermore, power relations shape all social ties and forms of collective life. In other words, family and friendship are themselves beset with numerous problems and should not be romanticised as some kind of idealised solution (c.f. Stanley, Deville and Montgomerie 2016, 81).

These caveats also emphasise the ways in which problems of debt are complex and differentiated by multiple forms of social positioning and inequality. The work of Money A+E helps us learn more about how financial issues take on a specific inflection within DECs. The different experiences of debt people have according to ethnicity is little researched in the UK context, despite clear evidence that ethnicity and poverty are intertwined. Asian, African and Afro Caribbean ethnic groups are the 'most likely to be in persistent poverty, that is, having less than 60 per cent of median income (before housing costs) in 3 of the last 4 years after taking the size and composition of households into account' (UK Government Cabinet Office 2018, 27). Persistent poverty means less opportunity to save and a greater need to borrow and is thus a better indicator of the likelihood of debt problems than the overall poverty rate. Approximately 1 in 4 children in households headed by people from an Asian background or those in the Other ethnic group were in persistent poverty, as were 1 in 5 children in Black households, compared to 1 in 10 White British households (UK Government Cabinet Office 2018, 27).

Low-paid work and unemployment are key factors shaping who becomes indebted. DEC families and individuals are more likely to be unemployed, and when in work, DEC individuals are disproportionately likely to be on a low income. 'White British workers earn an average of 3.8 per cent more, and the gap rises to 20 per cent for some ethnic groups. This means that ethnic minority groups affected by this pay gap face a higher risk of getting into debt' (Morris 2019, n.p.). 'Almost half of households in [Asian, African, Afro Caribbean or Other ethnic groups] had incomes in the bottom 40% nationally before housing costs were taken into account' (UK Government Cabinet Office 2018, 27). Lower levels of homeownership and the proportionately higher of renting are also factors that make these communities more likely to be in debt. 'The households most likely to rent social housing were in the African, Caribbean, Other Black, Bangladeshi, Irish, Arab and mixed groups (with the exception of the mixed White and Asian group)' (UK Government Cabinet Office 2018, 31). These ethnicity-based inequalities have been exacerbated by the Covid-19 pandemic (Money A+E 2020; Harker, Huq and Charalambous 2020).

Furthermore, organisations set up to help these marginalised communities may themselves face similar financial issues. Azumah (2019, n.p.) notes that:

> compared to the mainstream social sector, the Black, Minority, Ethnic (BME) third sector has been historically underfunded, and has faced a plethora of funding challenges. This includes being disproportionally affected by the government's reduction in grant funding since the onset of austerity measures. This is for two reasons. First, ethnic minority owned social organisations receive most of their funding from the government, and secondly, they are less likely to get funding from other grant making organisations. Voice4Change found that about 53% of BME third-sector enterprises receive a majority of their funding from government sources while they received only 3% of charitable funding and 2.3% of lottery grants in 2007.

While such statistics present evidence for the structural factors that shape the financial lives of DECs, there is a dearth of research about lived experiences of ethnicity and their impact in shaping money and debt. Evidence from Money A+E's practice suggests that within DECs there are strong normative ideas about who manages money that map onto age and gender. For example, one Black female service user suggests her money problems began after a relationship breakdown, because her father and then her male partner had always been in charge of her finances. There may be specific costs associated with practices such as weddings, through which debts are encumbered. There is a sense among staff that the austerity-driven necessity to borrow to afford the high cost of living in the UK has led to generational shifts in attitudes to becoming indebted. More research is needed in this area to complement nascent efforts to understand how contemporary lived finance emerges from experiences of racism and racialisation and the struggles to combat them (Kish and Leroy 2015; Bourne et al. 2018; Harker 2020).

It is also important to note that the structures and experiences of race and racism fold into other geographies of inequality such as gender, age and location. London has the highest poverty rates in the UK. The two boroughs Money A+E works in most intensively – Hackney and Newham – were the only boroughs in London with a poverty rate above 28 per cent in 2020. Rising poverty rates can be attributed to skyrocketing housing costs, low-paid and insecure work and changes to social security estimated to have resulted in 470,000 more people living in poverty in the UK between 2016 and 2020–21 (Azumah 2019).

Money A+E as pathway to prosperity

This chapter has argued that Money A+E's method of debt advice – working with and through family, peer and community relationships – offers a more robust alternative to debt advice services that work with, and reiterate, the debtor as an individual. This method acknowledges the ways in which debt problems are distributed through intimate relationships and that finance is always, already, social. This sociality also means debt and finance are always racialised. This concluding section argues that Money A+E's method might be thought about as not only capacitating people's ability to endure existing forms of finance, but also contributing in meaningful ways to the construction of more genuinely prosperous lives in East London.

Despite the centrality played by the concept of prosperity in visions of a common future (such as the United Nations Sustainable Development Goals), the concept remains under-studied and under-theorised (Moore and Woodcraft 2019). Conventionally equated with wealth and related measures such as gross domestic product, emerging conceptualisations rethink prosperity as a historically, geographically and culturally diverse set of ideas about what constitutes the good life (Moore 2015), which includes ideas and practices around in/equality, social cohesion, safeguarding the environment, education, health, decent employment and hope for the future (Moore and Woodcraft 2019). Consequently, prosperity is not a single goal, and while the challenges of prosperity may be global, the solutions will be contextually specific. Recent research in East London shows that strong social relationships are a key facet of local understandings of prosperity, alongside aspirations for a secure livelihood (Woodcraft and Anderson 2019). Therefore, methods of financial education, advice and support that are iterative, which is to say constantly expanding through existing social networks and ties, can be considered a key means through which people and communities can secure and enhance locally salient definitions of prosperity. Another way of thinking about this process is that Money A+E's way of working creates value in terms of intimate and community relationships, which form one part of a prosperous life in East London.

Furthermore, this pathway to inclusive and sustainable prosperity may well be particularly salient for the DECs that Money A+E primarily works with. The 2017 Race Disparity Audit (UK Government Cabinet Office 2018, 9) notes that

> the majority of people in each ethnic group also felt a sense of belonging to their local neighbourhood. This was similar across [all] ethnic groups, and manifested in a range of positive civic behaviours and attitudes. More than three quarters of people from each ethnic group felt that their local area is a place where people from different backgrounds get on well together: Black people reported the lowest levels and people from an Asian background reported very high levels. However, Black people – together with White people and people in the Other group – were the most likely to participate in some regular formal volunteering.

Creating local value by enhancing intimate and community relationships is thus likely to benefit all service users, regardless of race. However, the iterative nature of Money A+E's model, where service users become service providers, and the largely voluntary labour that underpins this practice, may be particularly suited to working in African and Afro Caribbean communities. Hence, while this chapter foregrounds Money A+E's method as potentially salient for addressing debt problems everywhere, it is crucial to recognise the ways in which this is a locally driven practice that draws on and benefits from contextually specific factors.

Notes

1 While this chapter was primarily authored by Harker and During, it benefitted from extensive comments from all the Money A+E staff. The authors would like to note the contributions made by Greg Ashby and Suzy Kirby in particular. We are also grateful for the detail and insightful comments provided by Amy Horton on an earlier draft.

2 The following is taken from the Money A+E website:

The term Diverse Ethnic Communities (DEC) refers to any and all ethnic communities.

We prefer to avoid terminology that uses colour to describe people, as this is not always accurate. We also prefer to avoid using continents to describe people, as this may group many culturally disparate people together. We believe that both of these options can lead to inaccurate labelling and stereotyping of people and communities.

We commit instead to describing people using their chosen nationality and/or country of origin wherever possible. We believe that this is more accurate and more respectful towards everyone with whom we work at Money A+E.

References

Azumah, C. 2019. *Supporting Diverse Ethnic Communities*. London: Money A+E. Accessed 17 June 2021. https://2bcaaa8d-c745-429e-b30c-1448d4080328.filesusr.com/ugd/ef4f34_c3c1cc40fa284da8bcd745345c20965d.pdf.

Barrett, C. 2019. 'Inside the UK's debt crisis', *Financial Times*. 26 April 2019. Accessed 17 June 2021. https://www.ft.com/content/1ea8527a-5464-11e9-91f9-b6515a54c5b1.

Barrett, T. 2019. 'The impact of the introduction of Universal Credit on advice agencies'. In *Problems of Debt: Explorations of life, love and finance*, ed. S. Kirwan, 63–78. Bristol: ARN Press.

Berglund, O. 2019. 'Resisting debt and evictions'. In *Problems of Debt: Explorations of life, love and finance*, ed. S. Kirwan, 90–8. Bristol: ARN Press.

Bourne, C., Gilbert, P., Haiven, M., and Montgomerie, J. 2018. 'Colonial debts, imperial insolvencies, extractive nostalgias', *Discover Society* 60: n.p.

Davey, R. 2019. 'Mise en scène: The make-believe space of over-indebted optimism', *Geoforum* 98: 327–34.

Davies, W., Montgomerie, J., and Wallin, S. 2015. *Financial Melancholia: Mental health and indebtedness*. London: Goldsmiths, University of London.

Dawney, L. 2019. 'On hypervigilant subjects'. In *Problems of Debt: Explorations of life, love and finance*, ed. S. Kirwan, 50–8. Bristol: ARN Press.

Deville, J. 2015. *Lived Economies of Default: Consumer credit, debt collection, and the capture of affect*. London: Routledge.

Gutierrez Garza, A. 2019. 'The two faces of debt'. In *Problems of Debt: Explorations of life, love and finance*, ed. S. Kirwan, 24–33. Bristol: ARN Press.

Harker, C. 2020. *Spacing Debt: Obligations, violence and endurance in Ramallah, Palestine*. Durham, NC: Duke University Press.

Harker, C., and Anderson, B. 2020. *Evaluating the Impact of Money Advice and Education's Work on Creating Prosperity: Preliminary report*. London: UCL Institute for Global Prosperity. Accessed 17 June 2021. https://www.ucl.ac.uk/bartlett/igp/sites/bartlett/files/money_advice_preliminary_report.pdf.

Harker, C., Huq, Z., and Charalambous, E. 2020. *Covid-19 as a Challenge to Prosperity: The case of Money A+E service users*. London: UCL Institute for Global Prosperity. Accessed 17 June 2021. https://www.ucl.ac.uk/bartlett/igp/sites/bartlett/files/covid_19_as_a_challenge_to_prosperity.pdf.

Harker, C., Sayyad, D., and Shebeitah, R. 2019. 'The gender of debt and space: Notes from Ramallah-Al Bireh, Palestine', *Geoforum* 98: 277–85.

James, D. 'In charge of your life'. In *Problems of Debt: Explorations of life, love and finance*, ed. S. Kirwan, 79–89. Bristol: ARN Press.

Jones, R. 2019. 'UK's problem debtors to get 60-day "breathing space"', *Guardian*. 19 June 2019. Accessed 17 June 2021. https://www.theguardian.com/money/2019/jun/19/uks-problem-debtors-to-get-60-day-breathing-space.

Jones, R. 2021. 'Complaints about guarantor loans rise by 3,000% in a year', *Guardian*. 3 March 2021. Accessed 29 November 2021. https://www.theguardian.com/money/2021/mar/03/complaints-about-guarantor-loans-rise-by-3000-in-a-year.

Karim, L. 2008. 'Demystifying micro-credit: The Grameen Bank, NGOs, and neoliberalism in Bangladesh', *Cultural Dynamics* 20 (1): 5–29.

Kirwan, S. 2019a. 'On "those who shout the loudest": Debt advice and the work of disrupting attachments', *Geoforum* 98: 318–26.

Kirwan, S. 2019b. 'Changing times for debt advice'. In *Problems of Debt: Explorations of life, love and finance*, ed. S. Kirwan, 129–39. Bristol: ARN Press.

Kish, Z. and Leroy, J. 2015. 'Bonded life: Technologies of racial finance from slave insurance to philanthrocapital', *Cultural Studies* 29 (5–6): 630–51.

Makortoff, K. 2019. 'Shares in lender Amigo plunge as regulatory crackdown looms', *Guardian*. 29 August 2019. Accessed 17 June 2021. https://www.theguardian.com/money/2019/aug/29/amigo-shares-regulatory-crackdown-loans-lending.

Mind. 2011. *Still in the Red: Update on debt and mental health*. London: Mind. Accessed 17 June 2021. https://www.mind.org.uk/media-a/4348/still-in-the-red.pdf.

Mind. 2020. 'Mind warns of "second pandemic" as it reveals more people in mental health crisis than ever recorded and helpline calls soar'. 13 November 2020. Accessed 17 June 2021. https://www.mind.org.uk/news-campaigns/news/mind-warns-of-second-pandemic-as-it-reveals-more-people-in-mental-health-crisis-than-ever-recorded-and-helpline-calls-soar/.

Money A+E. 2020. 'DEC/BAME groups hit harder by lockdown but benefited from financial education – UCL/Money A+E report'. 25 September 2020. Accessed 17 June 2021. https://www.moneyaande.co.uk/post/dec-bame-groups-hit-harder-by-lockdown-but-benefited-from-financial-education-ucl-money-a-e-report.

Money Advice Service. 2018. *Mapping the Unmet Demand for Debt Advice in the UK*. London: Money Advice Service. Accessed 17 June 2021. https://masassets.blob.core.windows.net/cms/files/000/001/064/original/Mapping_the_unmet_demand_for_debt_advice_in_the_UK.pdf.

Money and Mental Health. 2019. *The Money and Mental Health Manifesto 2019*. London: Money and Mental Health Policy Institute. Accessed 17 June 2021. https://www.moneyandmentalhealth.org/wp-content/uploads/2019/11/Money-and-Mental-Health-Manifesto-2019.pdf.

Moore, H. 2015. 'Global prosperity and Sustainable Development Goals', *Journal of International Development* 27 (6): 801–15.

Moore, H. and Woodcraft, S. 2019. 'Understanding prosperity in East London: Local meanings and "sticky" measures of the Good Life', *City and Society* 31 (2): 275–98.

Morris, N. 2019. 'The racial debt gap in the UK disproportionately affects black and Asian households', *Metro*. 30 November 2019. Accessed 17 June 2021. https://metro.co.uk/2019/11/30/the-racial-debt-gap-in-the-uk-disproportionately-affects-black-and-asian-households-11229187/.

Stanley, L., Deville, J., and Montgomerie, J. 2016. 'Digital debt management: The everyday life of austerity', *New Formations* 87: 64–82.

StepChange. 2020. *Problem Debt and the Social Security System*. Leeds: StepChange. Accessed 17 June 2021. https://www.stepchange.org/Portals/0/assets/pdf/social-security-mini-brief-report.pdf.

Sweney, M. 2021. 'Amigo Loans warns it will go bust unless it resumes lending', *Guardian*. 29 November 2021. Accessed 29 November 2021. https://www.theguardian.com/business/2021/nov/29/amigo-loans-warns-it-will-go-bust-unless-it-resumes-lending.

UK Government Cabinet Office. 2018. *Race Disparity Audit: Summary findings from the ethnicity facts and figures website*. London: UK Government Cabinet Office. Accessed 17 June 2021. https://assets.publishing.service.gov.uk/government/uploads/system/uploads/attachment_data/file/686071/Revised_RDA_report_March_2018.pdf.

Woodcraft, S. and Anderson, B. 2019. *Rethinking Prosperity for London: When citizens lead transformation*. London: UCL Institute for Global Prosperity. Accessed 17 June 2021. https://discovery.ucl.ac.uk/id/eprint/10080172/1/LPI_Report_single_140619_update.pdf.

10
The energy transition, indebtedness and alternatives

Charlotte Johnson

The transition towards a low-carbon society requires high levels of investment both in terms of finance and in terms of societal engagement. It offers an opportunity to collectively rethink the economy. In this chapter I focus specifically on decarbonising the UK's housing stock and discuss a number of different approaches being used to socialise the costs of the transition. First, I look at low-carbon heat networks and how these new infrastructural arrangements can create financial precarity as costs are passed on to residents. I then outline two alternative approaches in which mission-driven organisations work with community groups to redefine the possible forms of engagement in the transition and the value produced through decarbonisation. Carbon Co-op works on whole-house refurbishment, building local capacity and supply chains to help its members reduce household carbon emissions while also stimulating a local retrofit economy. Repowering London works to overcome financial barriers that prevent households accessing cheaper, greener local electricity by crowdsourcing investment in collectively owned solar photovoltaic (PV) arrays. Both organisations aim to align low-carbon financing with what communities value, supporting a more locally embedded, less extractive form of prosperity.

Costing the low-carbon transition

The aspiration for the UK's transition to net zero to create a more socially just energy system and sustainable way of life is tempered by an acknowledgement of the size of the challenge (HM Government 2020). Housing is one of the sectors that needs to become 'nearly completely decarbonised' by 2050 (Committee on Climate Change 2019). In the UK, 15 per cent of greenhouse gases (GHG) come from housing, particularly heating. Improving how energy is used in our homes is a priority (HM Government 2020, 99). Newly built housing needs to meet increasingly high energy performance standards, while existing homes need to be retrofitted with energy-efficiency measures (insulation, for example) and new low-carbon technologies (such as new types of heating, renewable generation and storage). The costs of decarbonising the UK's housing stock by 2050 are estimated to be £250 billion (Committee on Climate Change 2020).

How to appropriately socialise the cost of decarbonising the UK's housing stock is a live and complex issue. Housing is very diverse, and homes require different measures to be installed to bring them up to the highest energy performance standards and make use of the least carbon-intense energy available. The costs are also wide ranging. The same amount of money spent on two different homes will not deliver the same energy outcomes. For example, over half of UK homes were built before 1965, when the first basic energy performance criteria were introduced in building regulations (see Figure 10.1 below). Older construction methods and materials mean that many older buildings are designated as 'hard to retrofit'.

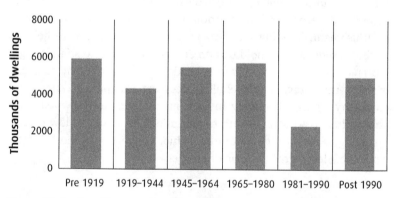

Figure 10.1 Dwelling age of UK housing stock (2017 data from BRE Group).

In addition, differences in tenure affect the legal rights and responsibilities of residents to alter the fabric of their homes and the energy-using appliances within. Most homes in the UK are owner occupied (see Figure 10.2). Owner occupiers can be freeholders who have responsibility for their own roofs, walls and windows, or leaseholders who are not able to make material alterations to their building's fabric. In England, 19 per cent of homes are leasehold, rising to over 30 per cent in some areas like London and the North West (Ministry of Housing Communities and Local Government 2020). Leaseholders pay ground rent and a service charge to a freeholder who uses this to make upgrades to the building envelope. There are also differences in the rented sector. For example, social renters are likely to own their kitchen appliances, while private renters are not.

A third area of complexity lies in the geographical differences. Local environmental conditions, housing density and building orientation can all affect the types of technologies or upgrades that it is appropriate to use, the costs of installing them and the scale of savings that a household might see on their running costs. For example, owners of a modern suburban house with a south-facing roof, garden and garage may find they can generate a lot of their own electricity. If the household can afford a rooftop solar installation, a ground source heat pump and a battery to store their electricity, they could significantly reduce how much power

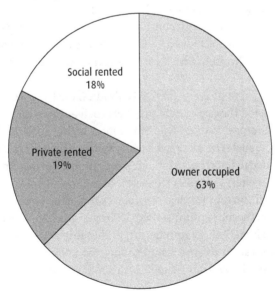

Figure 10.2 Dwelling tenure in the UK (2017 data from BRE Group).

they have to buy in from energy suppliers and potentially generate an income from these low-carbon assets by selling electricity or storage capacity back to the system. However, residents living in a flat in a city centre are likely to find their options much more limited, or subject to different regulations. For example, some cities are investing in heat networks, and residents in some urban neighbourhoods may find they have to connect to this infrastructure rather than generate their own low-carbon energy. Improving the energy performance of a home and its heating system, therefore, depends on a range of material, spatial and legal differences in housing type, as well as the occupants' financial ability and interest in making changes.

The UK government has used various mechanisms to generate the finance required to decarbonise housing,[1] with varying iterations and successes (Mallaburn and Eyre 2014). Support is tailored to different tenures and technologies. Central government funds have been made directly available to homeowners through grant schemes, financial incentives for renewable technologies and local authority funding for domestic refurbishment schemes. For example, the feed-in tariff subsidised renewable electricity generation and led to a large increase in domestic rooftop solar installations (McKenna, Pless and Darby 2018), although it has since been discontinued. Low-income households can receive free energy-efficiency measures through the Energy Company Obligation (Katris and Turner 2021). Both of these subsidies are funded through energy consumers' bills, and the fairness of this approach has been questioned, since it increases the energy bills of the lowest-income households, who contribute the least to UK GHG emissions.

In addition to direct grants and subsidies, the UK government has also encouraged the use of debt products such as loans and mortgages for the 'able-to-pay' market. One of the most highly publicised was the Green Deal, launched in 2013, which allowed homeowners to borrow the finance needed to improve their home's energy performance and pay this back via their energy supplier (Rosenow and Eyre 2016, 141). In theory, the energy bill savings for these customers should eventually cover the investment in the measures installed. However, the Green Deal failed in driving deep home energy retrofits largely because of the comparatively high interest rate it offered, and the fact the policy was designed to exclude the harder and more expensive retrofit measures (Rosenow and Eyre 2016).

Currently, the main products open to consumers are 'green mortgages' offered by a couple of high street banks, personal loans tied to specific products enabling consumers to spread the cost of a new boiler, for example, and equity release for homeowners aged over 55. The lack of financial products has been identified by the Green Finance Institute (GFI) as a major barrier to the decarbonisation of UK housing. The GFI was established with government backing in 2019 to address barriers to investment in decarbonisation. It argues for expanding the number and types of financial products available, from salary sacrifice schemes to 'Property Assessed Clean Energy (PACE)' financing which indebts a property and allows successive occupiers to take on the repayment (GFI 2020, 44).

At the core of many of the financial mechanisms being offered is the idea that improving the energy performance of a home is a good investment. It can reduce household outgoings, as occupants should not need to buy as much energy to keep their home warm or run their appliances. However, decarbonising housing does not always fall into this 'win–win' scenario, particularly when switching fuel type. Decarbonising domestic heating, for example, requires a major transition away from gas. Currently, 85 per cent of UK households use gas to heat their homes (Department for Business, Energy, and Industrial Strategy [BEIS] 2018a). The UK's reliance on natural gas stems from the discovery of natural gas fields in the 1960s and the subsequent investment in a national gas infrastructure. Today, the unit cost of gas is low in comparison to electricity, and it has a highly developed appliance manufacturing base, a supply chain and a skilled labour force. This means it is comparatively cheap and easy for a consumer to replace an old, inefficient gas boiler with a new, efficient one, and they are likely to recoup costs through improved performance. But this will not deliver the emissions savings required. To achieve a net zero home, gas heating systems need to be replaced with electric ones or by a heat network where a remote low-carbon heat source provides heat to a group of buildings (Rosenow et al. 2020). The costs associated with these changes are much higher, in part due to the less-developed manufacturing base, supply chains and labour force, as well as the need to create or reinforce distribution networks and the higher unit costs of electricity. Heat networks are a particular challenge because they require an entirely new infrastructure and energy market. The next section looks at some examples of heat network developments and how occupants have been financially impacted.

Heat networks and the work of Fuel Poverty Action

Heat networks have been identified as playing a role in the UK's climate strategy because they can provide low-carbon heating, particularly in densely populated urban areas where there are potential waste-heat sources and concentrated demand (HM Government 2020; BEIS 2018b). They are seen as a future-proof option, because once a heat network is constructed, the heat source can be replaced as more low-carbon technologies become available. But getting a heat network under the streets in a dense urban environment is a very expensive matter (BEIS 2018b) and networks 'require a minimum level of customers for a minimum period of time to be financially viable' (Citizens Advice 2016, 22). One of the approaches the UK has taken to support the development of heat networks is to use urban regeneration projects. Redevelopments provide an opportunity to create a new network, allowing the initial generation capacity and network to be installed and offering the potential to expand the network into neighbouring sites as decarbonisation plans ramp up.

A regeneration site offers the chance to materially re-landscape an area, but it is also a major investment opportunity that local authorities use to attract private finance to invest in the infrastructure. A heat network operator already knows the potential revenue base (i.e. all the flats being redeveloped) and is able to negotiate a long-term contract to supply the heat for the redevelopment. Housing developers build the homes with the appropriate domestic infrastructure and connections, and when households move in, they automatically enter into a contract with the heating provider. The financing of these networks therefore combines significant public and private sector investment, but also relies on the financial contributions of consumers, both in terms of homebuyers taking out a mortgage to buy a property on-site and in terms of future occupants' heating and hot water requirements, which are modelled as revenue for the energy company running the network. These contributions are not always made clear to occupants prior to moving in and can introduce new forms of precarity. This is an issue that the campaign group Fuel Poverty Action (FPA) has been working on for a number of years.

FPA's first big piece of advocacy around heat networks took place in 2017, and focused on the redevelopment of the Myatt's Field North estate in the borough of Lambeth (London and Hodkinson 2017). This was a large and complex regeneration project financed through a private finance initiative, led by a private company (Regenter) under a 25-year contract with the local authority. The project involved the demolition of

305 local authority homes (including 58 leaseholds), the construction of 355 new ones (including 53 local authority leasehold and five freeholds) and the construction of a private housing development of 503 new private leasehold homes (known as the Oval Quarter). A further 172 local authority homes were refurbished rather than demolished, although tenants and leaseholders were not able to choose whether their home would be one of the ones refurbished or demolished. The redevelopment also involved the construction of a new energy centre and heat network to supply all 980 new and refurbished homes with heating and hot water. Regenter subcontracted an energy company (E.ON) which then entered into a 40-year contract with the local authority to run the district heating system. The occupants of the refurbished and new homes all have a long-term contract with E.ON to supply their heat, with no option to switch provider.

The new heating infrastructure created a number of problems. It did not operate well: there were technical faults leading to intermittent supply and inconsistent temperatures, problems with metering and billing, and the customer service and general communication was found to be very poor. In cases of technical faults, households found it very hard to get issues investigated or resolved when different contracting parties refused to take on responsibility to fix different parts of the network. The most contentious issue was the contractual expectation for E.ON to provide 'affordable heat'. At the time (2017), the heating sector in the UK was not well regulated[2] and residents found it hard to get clarity about what they were being billed for. Different tenures were offered different tariffs and billed different amounts for the standing charge (the fixed fee that contributes to the network and operating costs). The local authority paid the standing charge for their tenants, but not for their leaseholders. To complicate matters further, there was a difference in the energy performance of the new-build and refurbished homes. Figure 10.3 illustrates the different costs the different occupants could face given their tenure and housing type. It uses the estimated consumption for a one-bed property as modelled by E.ON, which provided estimated annual consumption for the different flats, maisonettes and houses developed on the site. E.ON expected new one-bed flats on the development to use 3,499 kWh a year and refurbished one-bed flats to use 6,250 kWh a year, recognising that the energy performance of the new-builds should be higher than the refurbished flats.

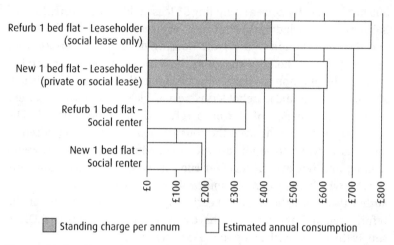

Refurb 1 bed flat – Leaseholder (social lease only)

New 1 bed flat – Leaseholder (private or social lease)

Refurb 1 bed flat – Social renter

New 1 bed flat – Social renter

£0 £100 £200 £300 £400 £500 £600 £700 £800

■ Standing charge per annum   □ Estimated annual consumption

Figure 10.3   Chart showing the different heating costs for residents on the Myatt's Field network (2016–17 tariff rates).

The amounts shown in Figure 10.3 are not actual bills: they show the theoretical amount residents can expect to pay based on the energy performance of their home and whether or not they are responsible for the standing charges. It shows that of all the residents in the redevelopment, the leaseholders living in refurbished local authority housing will in theory face the highest bills. These flats will have originally been rented to social tenants who at some point exercised their 'right to buy', looking for an affordable route into homeownership. The development also included 146 shared-ownership flats, a type of lease again designed for lower-income households to become owners of affordable homes. The shared-ownership flats are in the newly constructed 'Oval Quarter', and therefore the heating bills are estimated to be the second most expensive, at around £600 a year for a one-bed flat. Residents found their heating costs very high. FPA's report cites a resident in the new Oval Quarter flats commenting on her heating bill: 'My housemate and I are now paying more in heating bills in this flat than we did for both gas and electricity in our three-bed, poorly insulated Victorian terrace we were renting before moving here. How can this be right?' FPA rightly questions how affordable a home is, if the resident cannot afford to heat it.

Part of the issue was the high standing charges and the lack of clarity about what these charges covered. The UK's energy regulator publishes data on what is included in the standing charges for domestic gas and electricity consumers. It shows the proportion of the bill that goes towards paying for local and national distribution infrastructure, the environmental policies like the grants mentioned in the introduction to this chapter, and how much the utilities companies take in profit. In contrast, the proportions of the heat network's standing charge that go towards the generation technologies, the distribution network, the operating costs or the company's profits are not clear. Table 10.1 below shows the annual standing charges for 2016–17 and includes the different tariffs that E.ON began to offer to leaseholders. The table also shows the UK's national average gas standing charge and unit prices for that year, which are well below these figures. A heat network tariff and a gas tariff are not directly comparable. The gas figures do not include the cost of buying, installing and maintaining the boiler, which a homeowner has to take on when they use gas to heat their home. In contrast, the heat network figures may include some of the equipment in the home, but also a contribution to the broader costs of developing this new form of infrastructure, as well as the labour force and supply chains that need to be developed.

Although the gas and heat network tariffs in Table 10.1 do not include comparable costs, to residents they feel directly comparable. They have moved from a situation where they could shop around for the best available energy deals and had some control over their energy-related outgoings, to being tied into a 25-year contract with a monopoly supplier from whom they cannot disconnect. Even if they do not use heat, they are likely to have to pay standing charges and contribute to the sunk infrastructure costs. Leaseholders, particularly those low-income households for whom their home purchase was supposed to be a route to affordable ownership and financial security, may feel the only options available to them to avoid financial precarity are to choose a tariff with a lower standing charge and higher unit charge and then not heat their

Table 10.1 Tariff options for leaseholders in Myatt's Field North and Oval Quarter (2016/17) and UK average gas charges for 2016.

	Annual standing charge	Unit cost (p/kWh)
Heat network standard user	£402.68	5.14
Heat network low user	£96.91	14.53
Heat network high user	£458.62	4.31
*Average gas charges for 2017**	*£86.37*	*3.64*

*Data from Table 2.3.4 Average variable unit costs and standing charges for gas, from the Domestic Energy Prices data published by BEIS.

homes; to move out and rent their central London flat to a household who can afford high running costs; or to sell up altogether.

One of the major concerns for the residents and FPA was the lack of transparency around the billing and absence of accountability for the cost and service performance. This was compounded by the lack of regulation and monopolistic nature of networks, which mean that comparisons between heat networks are hard and collective bargaining is limited, particularly when differences in tenure create different liabilities. To counter this, FPA convened a heat network users' group, which allowed residents to come together and share experiences of managing the infrastructure and the providers, swap information on bills and tariffs and develop strategies for collective action and service improvement.

The first meeting was held in May 2017. We heard from residents experiencing a range of different issues and being pushed into financial precarity through their new heat networks. One of the first stories we heard was from residents of Pembroke Park in West London, an estate built in 2011 with a mix of social rented and shared-ownership flats.[3] Among a catalogue of technical faults and failing services, a lack of insulation meant it was hard to get the new homes to heat up and energy bills were high. In addition, technical problems with the metering had meant residents had not been billed in the first nine months of occupancy. Some had racked up hundreds of pounds of debt, and the heating provider was recouping this via their prepayment meters. Every time a resident added credit to their meter, some was allocated to pay in advance for heating, but part was automatically allocated to the debt payment. A tenant explained to FPA, 'I am now putting £50 a week on the prepayment meter and getting £32.50 of energy' (FPA 2017). Thirty-five per cent of each credit was taken to service a debt that had been accrued five years before. Loading debt on the heat meter is a stark illustration of what poor-quality housing does to its occupants' outgoings; it creates financial precarity by making it more expensive to create liveable housing conditions. This route into fuel poverty is compounded by the fact that the homes are on a heat network. This means residents are exposed to a lack of regulation and the consequences of poor public-sector contracting (Housing Ombudsman Service 2021). Residents receive high bills and have limited strategies to influence how much heat is required to heat their home or how much they pay for it, shouldering the costs of this low-carbon infrastructure and its poor governance.

At the meeting we heard about a different set of issues from residents of older estates that were being connected to new heat networks. The efficiency and economic feasibility of a network increases as more heat sources and heat users are connected. To meet national carbon targets, new networks ideally expand out of their regeneration sites and connect domestic and commercial properties in the surrounding areas to deliver further carbon savings. In the London Borough of Islington, the local authority has been championing network expansion and innovation, including pioneering the capture and reuse of waste heat from the London Underground (Islington Council 2020). They have been funding this work through a variety of sources, including the Greater London Authority and the European Union.[4] However, leaseholders also have to make a contribution when their estate is connected up. Some leaseholders from the Redbrick Estate in Old Street attended FPA's first heat network users' meeting. Each leaseholder had received a £22,000 service charge bill to cover the costs associated with connecting their home to the extending heat network. The leaseholders were expected to pay this within 5 years, or a maximum of 10 years with additional interest charges (FPA 2018). The Redbrick Estate was built in the mid-1970s and owned by the local council. This meant some leaseholders had originally been social tenants in the estate at that time, but had since bought their homes, and were now pensioners facing capital costs for infrastructure expected to last 25–50 years. The leaseholders in Redbrick who did not have the capacity to save £22,000 would be expected to borrow money or sell their property to pay for its upgrade. A Redbrick resident suggested that it would be more appropriate for the public sector to borrow the finance for the capital costs of the building and infrastructure improvements, and that leaseholders could contribute through their annual service charges over the full length of the life of the infrastructure.

The underlying logic of charging the leaseholders for 'improvement works' is that the leaseholders would benefit from an increase in their asset's value and could borrow against this asset. However, it is not always clear what can legitimately be included in the service charge or how the costs will be apportioned between social tenants, leaseholders and the landlord. It is hard for leaseholders to discuss the value of the work and whether they feel it is a good investment or that they will be able to experience any benefit. Given the very large bills involved in major works, 'legal disputes between block owners and flat owners are common' (Bright, Weatherall and Willis 2019). The contested nature of leaseholder bills for major works and energy improvement is a recognised barrier to the upgrading of the housing stock (Weatherall, McCarthy and Bright 2018).

FPA has worked with residents' groups to put pressure on local and central government, housing providers, building contractors and heat network operators to resolve the issues that residents face. They have helped residents challenge back billing and get some debt written off. They have succeeded in getting housing providers to investigate and add missing insulation. They have created a loose network of people active on the issue, and have been critical to ensuring that the legislation now being worked on is informed by the real-life experiences of residents. Further residents' meetings have been held on issues of pricing, outages, compensation and major repairs, now with the participation of central government civil servants. FPA recently published a second major report on a new-build development in Tower Hamlets (FPA 2021). More stringent regulations for heat networks are expected to be implemented in the UK. This will potentially resolve some of the issues occupants had with faulty service, non-transparent costs and poor practices such as back billing. However, residents' stories about their heat networks point to broader issues around socialising the cost of the low-carbon transition and economic precarity.

Some residents had not known they were going to be supplied by a heat network and feel they were duped into a long-term contract with a monopoly supplier. Others had known and were attracted by the green credentials of the development, with its heat network and energy-efficient homes. They were knowingly using their personal creditworthiness to take out a mortgage to invest in this new property. There is a genuine interest in the potential that is offered through the new decentralised infrastructure, in rethinking individual responsibility for the climate crisis, in critically engaging with the property market by choosing to buy a flat in a low-carbon development. Their anger is directed towards the organisations that have sold this rhetoric and then failed to deliver on it, or worse, failed to work with tenants and residents to grapple with what the problems are and how to resolve them. Rather than participants in the transition, tenants and residents become sources of income, either through their need to buy heat or their ability to raise finance. The relations established through the infrastructure individualise and distance residents from the collective action needed to make decentralised energy systems work, squandering the potential to engage people in the low-carbon transition.

Some alternative approaches to affording the transition

The potential for the low-carbon transition to create an alternative, socially just energy system is more than corporate greenwashing. In this section I present some examples of community-led action on housing and energy which look for alternative forms of financing and try to make low-carbon homes or low-carbon electricity accessible and affordable.

People Powered Retrofit

The first example is the People Powered Retrofit (PPR) project led by Carbon Co-op, a Manchester-based community benefit society. Carbon Co-op describes itself as 'an energy services and advocacy co-operative that helps people and communities to make the radical reductions in home carbon emissions necessary to avoid runaway climate change' (Carbon Co-op and URBED 2019). Its approach to the low-carbon transition is to build local capacity, recognising local assets and working with organisations that share its aims (Carbon Co-op 2017). The PPR project targeted the issue of owner-occupier refurbishment. As explained at the start this chapter, there have been a number of policy mechanisms to drive homeowner finance towards retrofitting their property. In response to the ongoing difficulties in delivering energy-efficiency measures, the Department for Business, Energy, and Industrial Strategy (BEIS) offered funding for demonstrators. Carbon Co-op, together with its construction partner URBED, received funding from central government to run a local retrofit demonstrator. Their approach was to put the householder at the centre of their work, helping occupants to first understand the energy performance of their home, then plan the retrofit measures that would make a difference. They pointed them towards finance if needed, helping them engage local contractors that could carry out the works and providing quality assurance.

PPR pioneered a determinedly bottom-up and holistic approach that uses 'assets that already exist at a neighbourhood scale, including local knowledge and relationships, quality workforce skills and supply chain networks, and local authority and community capital' (Carbon Co-op and URBED 2019). Their approach encompassed support for local contractors to develop specific retrofit skills and local supply chains. They also recognised the value of using social networks within neighbourhoods to build awareness of and support for a market to deliver the skills, technologies, confidence and quality work that can produce the carbon reductions needed. Their focus on homeowners means they viewed access to finance as a part of the solution. While they did not explicitly assess the risk of pushing people into precarious financial positions, they did stress the need to find appropriate financial products. Their research report signposted two lenders: the London Rebuilding Society, which works with 'over-50s homeowners, with properties needing significant works but who struggle to access traditional finance' and the Hook Norton Low Carbon group, which has a revolving £200,000 retrofit loan pot (Carbon Co-op and URBED 2019). 'Loans are typically £3,000–5,000 at 0–3 per cent interest, which doesn't aim to cover the full cost of works but rather to provide an incentive for action' (Carbon Co-op and URBED 2019). Based on the demonstration project, Carbon Co-op concluded that a bottom-up approach could create a viable market for deep retrofit works in the Greater Manchester area, and it continues to drive this approach.

Widening access to renewable energy

The final case study looks at the work of Repowering, a London-based industrial and provident society. One of the key energy injustices it targets is access to low-carbon generation, an issue that developed along with the UK's feed-in tariff for low-carbon generation. This guaranteed an income from low-carbon technologies, based on generation capacity. The initial rate was generous (50p/kWh), and by 2011 domestic solar PV installations reached a peak of 55,000 installations per month (McKenna, Pless and Darby 2018). However, occupants in multi-occupancy buildings, both tenants and leaseholders, typically could not benefit, because they had no legal responsibility for their roof. Repowering sought to address this by pioneering a model of community ownership and working with housing providers to lease roof space for a community-owned PV installation. In 2012 the organisation installed its first two arrays on social-housing estates after crowdsourcing the finance with a community share offering. Repowering helped establish renewable-energy community benefit societies (a type of co-operative), with each investing member receiving one vote in the society. Crowdsourcing finance for low-carbon generation assets became a fairly standard model for the community energy sector in the UK. The certainty of the income from the feed-in tariff meant groups had a future revenue stream that they could offer as a return to small-scale investors and use to resource a community fund for local projects. By 2017, Community Energy England (2017) was reporting an annual investment of £63.1 million from crowdsourced finance, in comparison to £47.5 million of loans for community-owned low-carbon generation. Repowering's model deviated from the norm in its ambition to deliver training opportunities to local young people and offer very small shares (from £5) to residents of the estates that would host the rooftop PV.

This model of developing community-owned low-carbon generation was challenged by the reduction of the feed-in tariff and then its removal in 2020 (Robinson and Stephen 2020). Repowering still supports community groups to develop generation projects, but it also works with technology firms and utility companies to design and run innovation trials. A recent project is a local energy market piloted with residents of the social-housing block that accommodated one of Repowering's first community-owned solar PV arrays. This new market is designed to optimise on-site use of the electricity produced by the array and generate bill savings for households in the building. Whereas the feed-in tariff meant communities earned income from exporting electricity to the grid, this local market allows residents to buy the solar output from their energy provider at below-market costs. Participating residents are allocated an equal share of the energy produced, and they can share or sell any energy they are not able to use at the time it is available to their neighbours via a peer-to-peer trading app designed by the utility (EDF Energy 2019). The project has also allowed a communal battery to be funded, increasing the amount of solar energy that residents use, as well as piloting an additional income stream by offering local grid balancing services to the electricity network operator (UK Power Networks 2019).

Repowering partakes in innovation trials to advocate on behalf of the communities it works with and develop a more democratic energy system. While renewable-energy generation is a core area of work, the organisation also has advice, advocacy and training services which help people access affordable energy and avoid debt. The innovation trials allow Repowering to put this understanding of lives lived in fuel poverty into new services designed by utilities companies and push for a more just transition.

Conclusion

Decarbonising the UK's housing stock means retrofitting the fabric and systems of its older buildings and developing local infrastructures that allow for optimal use of low-carbon energy. The costs of the technical solutions can be high, particularly when new systems are replacing long-established and regulated infrastructures. The upfront investment needed may not be recouped through reduced running costs. Decarbonisation therefore requires not only financial investment, but also engagement with the broader, non-financial value that decarbonisation delivers. In this chapter, I have presented three different approaches to this. In the case of the heat networks, where a household's future energy consumption and borrowing ability are seen as an income stream to attract private finance, 25-year contracts are used to lock in consumers, producing new forms of financial precarity. Technical problems are masked through individualising costs and liabilities, and the potential for people to actively support the transition is lost. These examples stand in sharp contrast to the other approaches described in this chapter.

The scale of the financial risk involved in developing a community-scale battery is not comparable to the much larger risk involved in developing a large heat network. However, I make the comparison to show the different ways of thinking about communities financially engaging with the low-carbon transition and the new forms of opportunity and precarity this opens up. Local solutions to decarbonisation are recognised as key to delivering on targets, but the rhetoric of local solutions does not mean they are necessarily socially embedded in that neighbourhood. This is a point made by Devine-Wright (2019), who argues that losing community engagement with local decarbonisation solutions risks undermining our ability to deliver the kinds of carbon reductions anticipated and needed. In this chapter I have shown two examples of organisations working to keep the community in view and facilitate collective action. Repowering champions the needs of the vulnerable and demands access to renewable energy for all households, regardless of tenure. It looks for investment from communities themselves and seeks to generate revenue for the community. Carbon Co-op is creating a groundswell of action and a viable market for retrofit, helping member households to dramatically increase the energy performance of their homes and decrease the emissions. Both approaches place an emphasis on local engagement that goes beyond recruiting people and seeks to develop new forms of value that are circulated locally.

Notes

1   The devolved governments of Scotland and Wales have used some other approaches not discussed here due to limited space.
2   Regulations are expected to be implemented by the current government.
3   Shared ownership is a government-backed 'help-to-buy' scheme where a homebuyer can purchase a proportion of a flat and rent the other proportion from the landlord.
4   The Bunhill heat network is part of the Celsius Project: https://celsiuscity.eu/about-us/.

References

Bright, S., Weatherall, D., and Willis, R. 2019. 'Exploring the complexities of energy retrofit in mixed tenure social housing: A case study from England, UK', *Energy Efficiency* 12 (1): 157–74.

Carbon Co-op. 2017. *Carbon Co-op Policy Manual Version 1.3 July 2017.* Manchester.

Carbon Co-op and URBED. 2019. *People Powered Retrofit: A community led model for owner occupier retrofit. Project report.* Manchester.

Citizens Advice. 2016. 'District heating networks: Analysis of information request, January 2016'. 20 January 2016. Accessed 27 January 2022. https://www.citizensadvice.org.uk/district-heating-networks/#!.

Climate Change Committee. 2019. *Net Zero: The UK's contribution to stopping global warming.* Accessed 27 January 2022. https://www.theccc.org.uk/wp-content/uploads/2019/05/Net-Zero-The-UKs-contribution-to-stopping-global-warming.pdf.

Climate Change Committee. 2020. *The Sixth Carbon Budget: The UK's path to net zero.* 9 December 2020. Accessed 27 January 2022. https://www.theccc.org.uk/wp-content/uploads/2020/12/The-Sixth-Carbon-Budget-The-UKs-path-to-Net-Zero.pdf.

Community Energy England. 2017. *Community Energy State of the Sector: A study of community energy in England, Wales and Northern Ireland.* Accessed 27 January 2022. https://communityenergyengland.org/files/document/280/1560344609_2017_CommunityEnergy-StateoftheSectorReport.pdf.

Department for Business, Energy and Industrial Strategy (BEIS). 2018a. *Clean Growth – Transforming heating: Overview of current evidence December 2018.* London, UK: BEIS.

Department for Business, Energy and Industrial Strategy (BEIS). 2018b. *Heat Networks: Ensuring sustained investment and protecting consumers.* London.

Devine-Wright, P. 2019. 'Community versus local energy in a context of climate emergency', *Nature Energy* 4 (11): 894–6.

EDF Energy. 2019. 'EDF empowers social housing residents to trade solar energy' [Press release]. Accessed 27 January 2022. https://www.edfenergy.com/media-centre/news-releases/edf-empowers-social-housing-residents-to-trade-solar-energy.

Fuel Poverty Action (FPA). 2017. 'Failing London district heating scheme in constituency of minister responsible for promoting district heating' [Press release]. Accessed 27 January 2022. https://www.fuelpovertyaction.org.uk/press-release/press-release-failing-london-district-heating-scheme-in-constituency-of-minister-responsible-for-promoting-district-heating/.

Fuel Poverty Action (FPA). 2018. *Written Evidence Submitted by Fuel Poverty Action to Leasehold Reform Inquiry.* Accessed 27 January 2022. https://www.fuelpovertyaction.org.uk/wp-content/uploads/2018/09/Response-to-leasehold-reform-inquiry.pdf.

Fuel Poverty Action (FPA). 2021. *Holding Feet to the Fire: Peabody tenants confront unaccountable heating and housing management.* Accessed 27 January 2022. https://www.fuelpovertyaction.org.uk/wp-content/uploads/2021/04/Peabody-tenants-confront-unaccountable-heating-and-housing-management.pdf.

Green Finance Institute. 2020. *Financing Energy Efficient Buildings: The path to retrofit at scale.* Accessed 27 January 2022. https://www.greenfinanceinstitute.co.uk/wp-content/uploads/2020/06/Financing-energy-efficient-buildings-the-path-to-retrofit-at-scale.pdf.

HM Government. 2020. *Energy White Paper: Powering our net zero future*. Accessed 27 January 2022. https://assets.publishing.service.gov.uk/government/uploads/system/uploads/attachment_data/file/945893/201215_BEIS_EWP_Command_Paper_Large_Print_Web.pdf.

Housing Ombudsman Service. 2021. *Cold Comfort: Spotlight on heating and hot water report*. Accessed 27 January 2022. https://www.housing-ombudsman.org.uk/wp-content/uploads/2021/02/Spotlight-on-heating-and-hot-water-report-final.pdf.

Islington Council. 2020. 'Bunhill Heat and Power: Cheaper, greener energy in Islington'. Accessed 1 March 2022. https://www.islington.gov.uk/environment-and-energy/energy/bunhill-heat-network.

Katris, A., and Turner, K. 2021. 'Can different approaches to funding household energy efficiency deliver on economic and social policy objectives? ECO and alternatives in the UK', *Energy Policy* 155 (August): 112375.

London, R., and Hodkinson, S. 2017. *'Not Fit for Purpose': Residents' experiences of E.ON's district heating system on the Myatts Field North Estate and Oval Quarter Development in Lambeth, London*. Accessed 27 January 2022. https://www.fuelpovertyaction.org.uk/wp-content/uploads/2017/04/MFN_OQ_EON_28-4-17_FINAL_EXEC.pdf.

Mallaburn, P. S., and Eyre, N. 2014. 'Lessons from energy efficiency policy and programmes in the UK from 1973 to 2013', *Energy Efficiency* 7 (1): 23–41.

McKenna, E., Pless, J., and Darby, S. J. 2018. 'Solar photovoltaic self-consumption in the UK residential sector: New estimates from a smart grid demonstration project', *Energy Policy* 118 (July): 482–91.

Ministry of Housing Communities and Local Government. 2020. *Estimating the Number of Leasehold Dwellings in England, 2018–19*. Accessed 27 January 2022. https://assets.publishing.service.gov.uk/government/uploads/system/uploads/attachment_data/file/898194/Leasehold_Estimate_2018-19.pdf.

Robinson, S., and Stephen, D. 2020. *Community Energy State of the Sector 2020*. Sheffield.

Rosenow, J., and Eyre, N. 2016. 'A post mortem of the Green Deal: Austerity, energy efficiency, and failure in British energy policy', *Energy Research & Social Science* 21 (November): 141–4.

Rosenow, J., Lowes, R., Broad, O., Hawker, G., Wu, J., Qadrdan, M., and Robert, G. 2020. *The Pathway to Net Zero Heating in the UK: A UKERC policy brief*. London.

UK Power Networks. 2019. 'Brixton residents first in UK to trial smart "flexible energy" project' [Press release]. Accessed 23 January 2022. https://www.ukpowernetworks.co.uk/internet/en/news-and-press/press-releases/Brixton-residents-first-in-UK-to-trial-smart-flexible-energy-project.html.

Weatherall, D., McCarthy, F., and Bright, S. 2018. 'Property law as a barrier to energy upgrades in multi-owned properties: Insights from a study of England and Scotland', *Energy Efficiency* 11 (7): 1641–55.

11

Conclusion: Transitioning to caring economies: what place for debt?

Amy Horton

To realise prosperity, we need to resolve related crises of debt, climate change and care. Increasingly, 'people can only afford to survive and thrive . . . through credit', yet debts often undermine both well-being and 'the very habitability of our planet' (see Harker, chapter 1, 3). However, as this book has demonstrated, there are many ways of financing prosperity by dealing with debt. Here I reflect on some of the key themes of the volume and add a focus on care.

The crisis of care involves our collective failure to ensure that we can meet our overlapping physical and emotional needs while properly supporting and valuing the work of care, which must be distributed fairly across different groups, in place of the current gendered and racialised divisions of labour (Dowling 2020; Raghuram 2019). Needing and providing care is now widely associated with indebtedness among disabled people and single parents, unpaid carers and care workers on poverty wages (Sepúlveda Carmona 2013; Ryan 2020). In contrast, caring economies would help to ensure that everyone had 'the support they need to live a good life and make a valued contribution' (In Control 2021) – including by guaranteeing that all of us have the resources to participate in caring for ourselves, each other and our environment. Visions for caring economies resonate with different communities' definitions of prosperity, which commonly highlight the need for 'secure and good quality livelihoods, good public services, a clean and healthy environment, planetary and ecosystem health, a political system that allows everyone to be heard, and the ability to have rich social and cultural lives' (Moore and Mintchev 2021, 3). Conceptually, too, ideas of prosperity echo ethical theories of care, in that both are concerned with 'knowledge about how to live a good life' (Tronto 1998, 15). According to the ethics of care, people must be understood not as isolated individuals but as social subjects who depend on each other and our environment for survival and well-being. This interdependence implies extensive forms of responsibility which connect different scales and institutions (Harris and Wasilewski 2004). Ethics of care offer a useful framework for analysing debt and working towards prosperous caring economies.

This chapter proceeds in three sections. First, it shows how debt and austerity undermine care. Austerity redistributes debt and produces a more uncaring welfare state. Gaps in collective provision are filled by intensified exploitation of the care workforce, additional unpaid care and greater household debt. In turn, debts can place greater strain on caring labour and relationships. At the macro-economic level, a reliance on private debt to stimulate the economy tends to deepen inequalities instead of fostering supportive interdependence. Drawing from the preceding chapters, we find a range of alternatives to austerity, as well as means of addressing existing debts. Closely related to austerity are tensions around debt, democracy and care. Rather than seeing care as a private matter, we need to recognise it as a shared responsibility that is essential to equality, and therefore democracy. Secondly, then, the chapter identifies how debt can be anti-democratic, including within mainstream efforts to 'democratise finance' by spreading access to services and asset ownership. Reflecting on examples from the rest of this volume and incorporating care ethics, I set out different interpretations of what democratising finance might mean, and how these can help to secure a wider range of values than those currently recognised in the market.

What role is there for debt in creating these more ethical economies? In seeking to challenge austerity, some commentators have adopted a relatively uncritical view of state debt – arguing that long-standing low interest rates and future growth mean that high levels of public debt can be taken on freely and viewed as a socio-economic investment. However, doing so risks locking high-income countries into a reliance on growth that is resource-intensive and incompatible with averting catastrophic climate change. The final section of the chapter therefore considers different approaches to financing a feminist 'just transition' to economies that are ecologically sustainable while addressing issues of poverty and gender inequality. It suggests debt-free public money (Mellor 2020) could play an important role in supporting caring economies.

How debt and austerity undermine care

Contradictions between debt and austerity, on the one hand, and prosperity, on the other, have been a key theme of this volume. This section reviews three major facets of this relationship in terms of their impact on care, and then outlines some of the alternatives presented throughout the book.

Austerity often follows the redistribution of debt from the private sector to the state, as in the bank bailouts during the 2008 financial crisis (French, Leyshon and Thrift 2009). The resulting burden on public finances has been used to justify significant cuts to vital social support. For example, the Bank Job project, based in northeast London, was devoted, in part, to fundraising for local services facing austerity, including a primary school and youth project (see Powell and Edelstyn, chapter 8). Funds have also been diverted away from critical services because of the costs of private finance for local government. As citizen debt audits have revealed, local authority borrowing has been subject to very high fees and interest payments in some of the UK's poorest areas. These costs of debt divert funds from critical services such as social care (one of the main expenditures for local government), which particularly harms low-income groups, racialised minorities, single parents, disabled people and women (see Malinen, chapter 2). Overall, debt can generate neglect rather than care and support. This places a greater burden on other, unpaid forms of care, such as volunteers running food banks (see Powell and Edelstyn, chapter 8; Elson 1992).

Austere welfare has also become a major source of debt at different scales. Alongside reduced public support for care, these debts strain the unequal capacities of households and other sites to provide care. Increasingly, debt is caused directly by the welfare system. The work of Money A+E has shown the significance of debts to the state – for example, council tax arrears – as benefits are cut while local governments raise taxes to compensate for reduced national redistribution (see Harker and During, chapter 9). All sorts of debts can further deplete caring capacities through anxiety or overwork. This is the dark side of the 'financialisation of social reproduction' – that is, giving individuals or families the responsibility for regenerating life (and with it, the labour force) by managing welfare through financial products such as private pensions, mortgages and student loans (Roberts 2016). Financialised social reproduction deepens socio-spatial inequalities, given the disparities in wealth, income, financial services and risk (Gardner, Moser and Gray 2020). Beyond the household, increasingly privatised welfare provision involves corporations that are themselves often loaded up with debt, thanks to deregulation, tax incentives and investment funds; such debts can shift risk to employers rather than investors, while the costs of servicing the debt detract from wages and resources available to service users. In the care home sector, for example, consequences include greater exploitation of paid care workers and more exclusionary services (Horton 2021).

Austerity also depletes public investment and undercuts consumer demand, so that private debt comes to play an increasingly important economic role. This macro-economic dependence on private debt tends to deepen inequalities instead of promoting supportive interdependence. Such dynamics are evident from efforts to stimulate the post-crisis austerity economy through quantitative easing, whereby 'Publicly subsidized credit flows through the banks to households, giving banks an easy and unrivalled profit source but loading up households with relatively expensive debts that they struggle to maintain because of politically imposed austerity' (see Montgomerie, chapter 6). Meanwhile, reduced funding for social housing, alongside house-price inflation underpinned by vast mortgage lending, has contributed to a growing private rented sector, where tenants face insecurity and often pay high rents (Ryan-Collins, chapter 7). Relying on extensive household debt to not only fund consumption but also stimulate the economy – in preference to government borrowing and investment – has been characterised as 'privatised Keynesianism', which is unstable and generates crises (Crouch 2009).

Instead, contributors to this volume have argued for a *de-privatisation* of debt as a step towards more caring economies. De-privatising debt requires destigmatising debt as a personal issue by recognising it as a common experience that is generated by specific economic arrangements. It also involves shifting responsibility for welfare and investment from private households to collective actors that are better able to influence economies and bear risk. Among the solutions here are progressive taxation and better use of governments' ability to borrow at preferential rates (see Malinen, chapter 2). However, state borrowing should not be used to socialise the costs of avoidable crises caused by financial markets. Measures are needed such as regulation to prevent real estate speculation, which sucks household incomes into housing costs; instead, governments should ensure that money is channelled into valuable economic activities (see Ryan-Collins, chapter 7). Changes at these scales would reduce the risk of households falling into problem debt and help protect capacities for care. Where credit is needed, regional and community-based institutions can provide alternatives to predatory lending. For example, credit unions ensure that those excluded from commercial banking can access finance; any profits are reinvested or shared with those members rather than external shareholders (see Groombridge, chapter 4). Similar forms of solidarity are found in the work of social enterprises and faith organisations that are building 'critical financial capability' among Diverse Ethnic Communities, in order to help people to manage their finances and debts through mutual support. These approaches treat us as relational, caring subjects rather than isolated individual debtors (see Harker and During, chapter 9; Mladin, chapter 3).

There are also many ways to deal with the build-up of existing debt. Bankruptcy law could be reformed to make it more accessible and less punitive (Spooner, chapter 5). Beyond the individual scale, unrepayable debt can be cancelled for multiple borrowers at once (see Mladin, chapter 3; Powell and Edelstyn, chapter 8). Short of cancellation, publicly subsidised credit could be extended beyond banks and corporations to provide significant interest-free refinancing for households (see Montgomerie, chapter 6). And to finance the green transition, instead of imposing the long-term costs of interventions on low-income residents, community finance can be raised (see Johnson, chapter 10). These are means of dealing with debt that prioritise the well-being and caring capacities of debtors.

Democratising finance for more ethical economies

Tensions between debt, austerity and care also damage democracy. Democracy and care are interdependent because access to care and support for caregivers are fundamental to equality (Kittay 1999; Tronto 2013). This volume has identified multiple anti-democratic dimensions of debt, as well as presenting different approaches to democratising finance. Here, ethics of care are used to deepen this analysis.

Debt can be anti-democratic when it is taken on by public bodies without public scrutiny or if citizens have insufficient influence over the terms and purpose of the borrowing. It is also undemocratic when creditors' interests are prioritised over all else – including the human rights of debtors – in spite of the unequal capacity of creditors and debtors to bear risk. For example, in the context of austerity, local authorities were sold complex financial products and residents were denied information about these high-cost contracts, let alone a say over this risk taking, which drained millions from councils' already depleted budgets for vital services (see Malinen, chapter 2). Giving precedence to creditor rights over human rights, and allowing lenders to dominate and discipline government spending, has been characterised as a 'creditocracy' (Ross 2014; Soederberg 2005).

Paradoxically, this vision of debt as anti-democratic has run alongside efforts to 'democratise' finance by some of the very institutions that uphold the primacy of repayment as a moral and legal imperative. How can we unravel these different meanings of democracy? One interpretation emerges from the agenda for financial inclusion, where 'democratising finance' refers to *access* to financial products and services. In the Global South, this has meant extending formal financial services to those previously deemed too remote or poor to constitute a profitable market segment, most famously through micro-finance and mobile banking (Kirwan 2021). Such services have been promoted with gusto by the international financial institutions which have overseen austerity programmes that stripped back or stymied welfare states and pushed households into more individualised, financialised livelihoods. Their interventions have been criticised for failing to value existing, self-organised forms of saving, lending and investing (Shenaz Hossein 2017). In the Global North, broadly speaking, financial inclusion policy has also aimed to incorporate the 'under-served' – including those historically excluded by racist institutions (Prabhakar 2021). However, across different geographies, inclusion has often been exploitative, with new customers offered high-cost, high-risk finance and only partial access to financial services and products – for example, less profitable micro-savings have been less widely available than micro-credit (Kar and Schuster 2016). Democratising finance has also been extended to encompass *ownership* of assets – as in the promotion of a 'shareholding democracy' through the privatisation of state-owned companies under Margaret Thatcher's 1980s UK government. Property ownership is, according to Conservative MP John Redwood (1988), 'the economic expression of democracy', promising 'the democracy of the marketplace'. One pound, one vote.

Alternative interpretations suggest very different approaches to democratising finance compared to this agenda (Berry 2015). First, those who have been financially excluded need to be relieved of debts that are unrepayable or that were unjustly lent. This reflects an insistence within care ethics on the importance of relationships of responsibility and contextual decision making, which must be responsive to differing needs instead of applying universal rules to people as identical individuals of equal power (Bartos 2019). Unjust or irresponsible debts must be cancelled, or at least radically restructured, without condemning borrowers to punitive costs or exclusion (see Mladin, chapter 3; Spooner, chapter 5; Montgomerie, chapter 6). Access to finance should be on equal or preferential terms – like the terms offered by credit unions, which themselves require support from government to develop an adequate capital base (see Groombridge, chapter 4). People also need a genuine choice of appropriate financial services, such as banking that is compliant with Islamic prohibitions on interest (Kuran 1995). And choices outside finance should be expanded. For example, some Muslim students in the UK are excluded from interest-bearing student loans, but simply incorporating them into the existing student finance system would just extend huge debts to more graduates – and British Muslims are more likely to face poverty than other groups (Heath and Li 2015). Instead, more sustainable approaches, such as those based on progressive taxation, could be adopted.

Second, democratising ownership implies expanding different forms of organisation, such as member-owned credit unions, co-operatives and proper public involvement in decisions about state finances (see Malinen, chapter 2; Mladin, chapter 3; Groombridge, chapter 4; Johnson, chapter 10). These can foster supportive relationships and tackle power disparities, in line with ethics of care. For example, community benefit societies can issue shares on a one-member, one-vote basis, which means that wealth does not determine power among an institution's owners (see Johnson, chapter 10). The scope for addressing institutional racism is greater where stakeholders have more control.

Third, democracy demands that all those affected not only have rights to financial access and ownership, but also the power to influence decisions and participate in controlling how finance is created, distributed and used. Much of the work profiled in this volume has been about opening up finance to let the light in, to change how we feel about it and to show that debt is far more malleable than it appears: it is a relation of power that can be challenged (Graeber 2011). Such practices, like ethics of care, acknowledge that people are emotional, embodied subjects in relationship with others. Exposing debt as a common experience and a social relation is part of the work of Money A+E. Its approach, in Newham and other parts of London, recognises that people depend on social networks and, often, on informal financial help from family and friends, locally and transnationally. These relationships are trusted conduits for knowledge and skills and, equally importantly, emotional support. In the community mentoring scheme, there is no hard divide between those with experiences of problem debt and those offering guidance on how to deal with it; instead, lived expertise is harnessed. Some similarities can be observed in the Bank Job project, where people experienced producing money. By participating, members of the community learned about where money comes from, questioned what generates value and helped to write off distressed loans. The shared experience of creative experimentation and humour dragged debt out from the shadows – where many of us struggle with its burden, often alone and ashamed – to tackle it together. The project generated a sense of relief, financial resources, learning, art and 'the chance to make history'. The fact that this broad 'return on investment' proved so appealing to thousands of participants reflects the need for democratic finance to serve a range of values. The same point emerges from considering how to fund renewable energy and housing retrofits: 'The upfront investment needed may not be recouped through reduced running costs. Decarbonisation therefore requires not only financial investment, but also engagement with the broader, non-financial value that decarbonisation delivers' (see Johnson, chapter 10). This echoes the concept of a 'community economy return on investment' proposed by the feminist economic geographers J. K. Gibson-Graham, where returns include greater well-being at different scales, ecological benefits and increased collectively controlled surplus.

A concern with returns and values beyond direct financial gain raises ethical questions about what forms of return and values we want. To counter the potential for debt to be a 'domineering, enslaving, and ultimately deadly force', there is a need for an 'individual and social ethics of debt forgiveness', according to Mladin (see chapter 3). Examples of how this might be applied through political, fiscal and legal forms were presented by Malinen, Montgomerie and Spooner. The explosion of £1.2 million of distressed debt in the 'Big Bang 2' (see Powell and Edelstyn, chapter 8) was designed as an emancipatory 'ethical spectacle' (Duncombe 2007), evoking emotion and symbolism to rework how we think and feel about debt. More ethical forms of finance are offered by the credit unions profiled (see Groombridge, chapter 4) or community share offers (see Johnson, chapter 10). These aim to recirculate wealth within particular institutions and places, rather than it being extracted and concentrated among the more powerful market actors. They seek to support and foster relationships (see Mladin, chapter 3) instead of treating people as atomised, indistinct subjects – who interact only through voluntary, contractual exchanges. Understanding people as interdependent and looking to enhance the quality of our relationships is at the heart of ethical approaches centring on care. The next section explores the role of debt in financing an economy that prioritises care.

Can debt finance a feminist 'just transition'?

Multiple crises – of debt, climate change and our ability to meet our needs for care – demand economic transformations (Mazzucato 2020). With the Intergovernmental Panel on Climate Change signalling 'code red' for humanity (United Nations 2021), the interdependence of society and wider nature is starkly apparent. Our survival and prosperity demand urgent action: a 'just transition' to a low-carbon economy, which sustains livelihoods, including for those formerly employed in fossil fuel industries, as well as promoting climate justice by, for example, addressing energy poverty (Rosemberg 2010; Newell and Mulvaney 2013; Johnson, this volume). Feminist critiques have challenged visions for a green transition that focus only on male-dominated employment in industrial sectors (Bauhardt 2014). Recognition and support must also be afforded to the low-carbon, but undervalued, work of caring for people and the environment, which is disproportionately carried out by women, including migrants and people of colour (Bhattacharya 2019). Take the case of care for older people in England. This is a vast and growing area of employment in the context of an ageing population, but one in which the average care worker is paid barely above the legal minimum wage. Subject to deep austerity in the post-2008 period, the sector has one of the highest rates of staff vacancies and turnover across the economy. Many care companies are heavily indebted and at risk of collapse. More than a million people in need of care are left without it (Horton 2019). Instead, we need a 'world built on a feminist ethic of care, a care-full community economy', which prioritises community and environmental well-being across interdependent places. Core to this would be a 'politics of *increasing* and *redistributing* care work' (Dombroski, Healey and McKinnon 2018, 103), so that care is not neglected or seen as a marker of low social status, viewed as 'dirty work' or 'women's work' (Anderson 2000).

There are multiple proposals for addressing the interlinked crises of climate, debt and care. Some focus on freeing up time, space and energy for the essential work of caring for people and planet outside markets. This could involve redistributing and reducing hours of paid work and supporting care through a universal basic income or 'care income' (Barca

2020). Space and resources could be claimed through expanding the commons – the 'physical resources, knowledges, and cultural practices that are distinct from private property in that access, use, benefit but also responsibility and care are widely distributed' (Dombroski, Healey and McKinnon 2018, 105; Barbagallo and Federici 2012). More extensive services could offer greater professional care (Coote and Percy 2019). Another proposal is a feminist Green New Deal. Invoking the 1930s stimulus deployed in the United States to mitigate the Depression, a Green New Deal would involve significant spending to develop renewable energy and energy efficiency. A feminist version would also include funding for 'social infrastructures' – the places and labour required to support care, education and other activities essential to reproducing life (Cohen and MacGregor 2020).

While some of these changes could reduce reliance on markets and money, financial resources would still be required. Where should the funding come from? One view is that we should pursue green growth, in which economic activity and energy consumption are decoupled from greenhouse gas emissions, so that economies can expand without causing further harm to the climate. Green growth would, according to its defenders, avoid shrinking the economic base that is needed to finance the transition – as well as the political opposition that cuts to incomes would provoke (Pollin 2018). Contrary to scaremongering about the unaffordable costs of transition, it is argued that spending on green growth would ultimately pay for itself through increased economic output instead of costly climate chaos. As such, it can represent a form of social investment (Cohen and MacGregor 2020). However, proponents of 'degrowth' argue that high-income nations (and particularly high-income groups within them) cannot continue to pursue growth while simultaneously reducing emissions at the rate required to keep global temperature rises at agreed levels; they also argue that the scale of resources required for ever-growing green technologies (such as land and minerals) cannot be sustained (Hickel 2020).

Some promote the use of public-sector borrowing and other low-cost credit to finance a just transition (Pollin 2018). The Covid-19 pandemic may have triggered changes in attitudes towards both care and debt: it has exposed the importance of care and led to a greater acknowledgement of care work, while governments that had previously embraced austerity rolled out significant interventions to mitigate the damage of lockdowns. Facing familiar refrains about excessive state debt, opponents of austerity have pointed out that some governments could borrow at extremely low long-term interest rates, as investors desperately sought the least risky assets amid a huge downturn (Ascari et al. 2020). Debts, it was argued, could gradually be paid off and their scale would matter less as economies expanded. However, this sanguine view of sovereign debt is predicated on future growth. With emissions-intensive economies, growth will exacerbate the climate emergency. Yet efforts to slow or reverse growth for environmental reasons also risk negative reactions in financial markets: if debt repayment seems less assured, creditors can raise the cost of borrowing and investors may withdraw capital, deepening a downward spiral in government revenues and financing costs (Bailey 2020).

Alternatively, taxation – including of carbon – could be used to finance transition. However, reducing growth would not only change the dynamics of debt-based financing, but would also have implications for tax revenues. As Bailey (2020, 6) argues, 'any suppression of economic activity – for that is what GDP is a measurement of – is a suppression of taxable economic activity, and there are thus consequences for the "tax take"'. These claims can be nuanced. Degrowth would target the most ecologically destructive and least socially necessary forms of production, which disproportionately serve the highest-income groups, rather than seeking an overall shrinkage of economies (Hickel 2020). Gross domestic product is, in any case, only a partial measure of economic activity (only covering monetary transactions) – so it excludes the extensive and vital non-capitalist forms of meeting our needs, such as unpaid care and volunteering (Gibson-Graham 2014); if greater financial support were extended to these activities (for example, through a basic income), then they could generate some tax revenues. Further, the idea that tax revenues closely reflect high rates of private profit is complicated by tax-avoidance practices, which have allowed companies such as Amazon to accumulate vast sums and billionaires to become wealthier than ever (Collins, Ocampo and Paslaski 2020). Nevertheless, it is clear that a just transition would have profound effects on tax revenues.

All of these approaches are premised on unsustainable growth and debt. Moreover, growth and the size of economies are not closely correlated with well-being, life expectancy or education, particularly in wealthier countries; the distribution of resources and the extent of inequality are crucial (Wilkinson and Pickett 2010). Targeting growth as a proxy for prosperity is a flawed approach – and one that is leading to climate catastrophe (Jackson 2009). Approaching social spending as 'investments' also risks commodifying and quantifying services and relationships that cannot be properly valued in this way (Dowling 2017). Yet if there is a role for the state in coordinating the transition, it will face a trilemma, at least in higher-income nations (Bailey 2018): how to reconcile an interventionist state with both the constraints of state financing and an ambition for 'postgrowth' economies.[1]

A different approach involves the generation of debt-free public money. Debt-free public money is an alternative to bank-issued money, which is always created as interest-bearing capital in the loans and bonds issued by banks, and which accounts for almost all of the money that is now in circulation in countries such as the UK. This 'debt-based money' is, according to Mary Mellor, 'socially, politically, ecologically and economically unsustainable' (2020, 126) because it serves only the most profitable concerns, undermines public expenditure, drives growth rather than sufficiency and leads to financial crises. In place of interest-bearing credit, Mellor advocates the creation of debt-free public money through direct expenditure by states. That spending could be democratically controlled through practices such as participatory budgeting. To prevent inflation, an independent monetary authority could recommend the required level of taxation. Existing, unjust debts could also be challenged, for example through debt audits (Bailey 2018; Malinen, chapter 2). Such proposals are anathema to advocates of independent central banks and free markets. Yet central banks do not conform to their non-interventionist ideal, and in fact play a major role in subsidising privately issued debt to the benefit of financial institutions. They have had to guarantee debts created by private banks – as in the huge bailouts in 2008 (Mellor 2020). Many central banks have undertaken quantitative easing programmes, which have extended vast credit to private banks, exacerbating inequality by inflating the prices of assets owned mostly by the wealthiest groups, while failing to really boost productive investment – let alone generating the kinds of changes needed for a just transition (House of Lords Economics Affairs Committee 2021). As Mellor (2020, 125) argues:

> While commercial views of money will always stress value in money terms as profit (money invested to make more money), social and public forms of money can address outcomes in terms of social and public benefit . . . While commercial value is judged in the marketplace, social value will be judged in terms of personal relationships, while public value can be judged at the ballot box or in public debate . . . Rather than profit in the market, public money could enable ecologically sustainable sufficiency provisioning. Debt-free public money could be created and used to fund caring activities on a not-for-profit basis.

Conclusion

This vision of debt-free public money reflects concerns for relationships, democracy and sustainability that are at the heart of caring economies. Although public funding and regulation can be essential and can allow larger-scale change (see Groombridge, chapter 4; Montgomerie, chapter 6), the groups and ideas presented here are working to democratise finance at the community scale. Many of the approaches are bottom-up, reflecting the needs of those without significant institutionalised power. For Bank Job, inspiration travelled from debt-resistance movements in the US, on to an unused building in outer London, and then flowed on through the book, film and reporting of the project (see Powell and Edelstyn, chapter 8). Debt audits in the UK, Greece and Spain have followed Ecuador's example of rejecting illegitimate debts (see Malinen, chapter 2). Credit unions have been established by immigrants to the UK from Caribbean nations (see Groombridge, chapter 4). The geography of efforts to democratise debt and value care is decentralised and transnational. As this book has shown, ideas and practices are proliferating that expose and challenge how debt undermines care, democracy and prosperity – and these are collectively working towards a just transition towards caring economies.

Notes

1   On the constraints facing countries in the Global South, see Gabor 2021. On decolonial approaches to degrowth, see, for example, Nirmal and Rocheleau 2019.

References

Anderson, B. 2000. *Doing the Dirty Work? The global politics of domestic labour.* London: Zed Books.

Ascari, G. et al. 2020. 'Economists urge BBC to rethink "inappropriate" reporting of UK economy', *IPPR*. Accessed 30 November 2020. https://www.ippr.org/blog/economists-urge-bbc-rethink-inappropriate-reporting-uk-economy.

Bailey, D. 2020. 'Re-thinking the fiscal and monetary political economy of the green state', *New Political Economy* 25 (1): 5–17.

Barbagallo, C., and Federici, S. 2012. 'Introduction – care work and the commons', *The Commoner Journal* 15: 1–21.

Barca, S. 2020. 'Within and beyond the pandemic: Demanding a care income and a feminist Green New Deal for Europe', 7 April 2020. Accessed 10 April 2020. https://undisciplinedenvironments.org/2020/04/07/within-and-beyond-the-pandemic-demanding-a-care-income-and-a-feminist-green-new-deal-for-europe/.

Bartos, A. E. 2019. 'Introduction: Stretching the boundaries of care', *Gender, Place and Culture* 26 (6): 767–77.

Bauhardt, C. 2014. 'Solutions to the crisis? The Green New Deal, degrowth, and the solidarity economy: Alternatives to the capitalist growth economy from an ecofeminist economics perspective', *Ecological Economics* 102: 60–8.

Berry, C. 2015. 'Citizenship in a financialised society: Financial inclusion and the state before and after the crash', *Policy and Politics* 43 (4): 509–25.

Bhattacharya, T. 2019. 'Three ways a Green New Deal can promote life over capital', *Jacobin*. 6 October 2019. Accessed 27 January 2022. https://jacobinmag.com/2019/06/green-new-deal-social-care-work.

Cohen, M., and MacGregor, S. 2020. *Towards a Feminist Green New Deal for the UK*. London: Women's Budget Group.

Collins, C., Ocampo, O., and Paslaski, S. 2020. *Billionaire Bonanza 2020: Wealth windfalls, tumbling taxes, and pandemic profiteers*. Washington, DC: Institute for Policy Studies.

Coote, A., and Percy, A. 2019. *The Case for Universal Basic Services*. Cambridge: Polity.

Crouch, C. 2009. Privatised Keynesianism: An unacknowledged policy regime, *British Journal of Politics & International Relations* 11 (3): 382–99.

Dombroski, K., Healy, S., and McKinnon, K. 2020. 'Care-full community economies'. In *Feminist Political Ecology and the Economics of Care: In search of economic alternatives*, ed. C. Bauhardt and W. Harcourt, 99–115. Abingdon: Routledge.

Dowling, E. 2017. 'In the wake of austerity: Social impact bonds and the financialisation of the welfare state in Britain', *New Political Economy* 22 (3): 294–310.

Dowling, E. 2020. *The Care Crisis: What caused it and how can we end it?* London: Verso Books.

Duncombe, S. 2007. *Dream: Re-imagining progressive politics in an age of fantasy*. New York, NY: OR Books.

Elson, D. 1992. 'From survival strategies to transformation strategies: Women's needs and structural adjustments'. In *Unequal Burden: Economic crises, persistent poverty and women's work*, ed. L. Benería and S. Feldman, 26–48. Boulder, CO: Westview Press.

French, S., Leyshon, A., and Thrift, N. 2009. 'A very geographical crisis: The making and breaking of the 2007–2008 financial crisis', *Cambridge Journal of Regions, Economy and Society* 2 (2): 287–302.

Gabor, D. 2021. 'The Wall Street Consensus', *Development and Change* 52: 429–59.

Gardner, J., Moser, K., and Gray, M. (eds). 2020. *Debt and Austerity: Implications of the financial crisis*. Cheltenham, UK: Edward Elgar Publishing.

Gibson-Graham, J. K. 2014. 'Rethinking the economy with thick description and weak theory', *Current Anthropology* 55 (9): 147–53.

Graeber, D. 2011. *Debt: The first 5,000 years*. London: Melville House Publishing.

Harris, L. D., and Wasilewski, J. 2004. 'Indigeneity, an alternative worldview: Four R's (relationship, responsibility, reciprocity, redistribution) vs. two P's (power and profit). Sharing the journey towards conscious evolution', *Systems Research and Behavioral Science* 21 (5): 489–503.

Heath, A., and Li, Y. 2015. 'Review of the relationship between religion and poverty' (CSI Working Paper 2015-01).

Hickel, J. 2020. 'What does degrowth mean? A few points of clarification', *Globalizations*, https://doi.org/10.1080/14747731.2020.1812222. [Online first.]

Horton, A. 2019. 'Financialization and non-disposable women: Real estate, debt and labour in UK care homes', *Environment and Planning A: Economy and Space*. https://doi.org/10.1177/0308518X19862580 [Online first.]

Horton, A. 2021. 'Liquid home? Financialisation of the built environment in the UK's "hotel-style" care homes', *Transactions of the Institute of British Geographers* 46: 179–92.

House of Lords Economics Affairs Committee. 2021. *Quantitative Easing: A dangerous addiction?* London: House of Lords.

In Control. 2021. 'About Us', *In Control*. 2021. Accessed 23 August 2021. https://in-control.org.uk/what-we-do/.

Jackson, T. 2009. *Prosperity Without Growth: Economics for a finite planet*. London: Earthscan.

Kar, S., and Schuster, C. 2016. 'Comparative projects and the limits of choice: Ethnography and microfinance in India and Paraguay', *Journal of Cultural Economy* 9 (4): 347–63.

Kirwan, S. 2021. *Financial Inclusion*. Newcastle, UK: Agenda Publishing.

Kittay, E. F. 1999. *Love's Labor: Essays on women, equality and dependency*. New York: Routledge.

Kuran, T. 1995. 'Islamic economics and the Islamic subeconomy', *Journal of Economic Perspectives* 9 (4): 155–73.

Mazzucato, M. 2020. 'Capitalism's triple crisis', *Social Europe*. 9 April 2020. Accessed 10 April 2020. https://socialeurope.eu/capitalisms-triple-crisis.

Mellor, M. 2020. 'Care as wellth: Internalising care by democratising money'. In *Feminist Political Ecology and the Economics of Care: In search of economic alternatives*, ed. C. Bauhardt and W. Harcourt, 116–30. Abingdon: Routledge.

Moore, H., and Mintchev, N. 2021. *What Is Prosperity?* London: Institute for Global Prosperity.

Newell, P., and Mulvaney, D. 2013. 'The political economy of the "just transition"', *The Geographical Journal* 179: 132–40.

Nirmal, P., and Rocheleau, D. 2019. 'Decolonizing degrowth in the post-development convergence: Questions, experiences, and proposals from two Indigenous territories', *Environment and Planning E: Nature and Space* 2 (3): 465–92.

Pollin, R. 2018. 'Degrowth vs a Green New Deal', *New Left Review* 112: 5–25.

Prabhakar, R. 2021. *Financial Inclusion: Critique and alternatives*. Bristol: Policy Press.

Raghuram, P. 2019. 'Race and feminist care ethics: Intersectionality as method', *Gender, Place & Culture* 26 (5): 613–37.

Redwood, J. 1988. *Popular Capitalism*. London: Routledge.

Roberts, A. 2016. 'Household debt and the financialization of social reproduction: Theorizing the UK housing and hunger crises', *Research in Political Economy* 31: 135–64.

Rosemberg, A. 2010. 'Building a just transition: The linkages between climate change and employment', *International Journal of Labour Research* 2 (2): 125–61.

Ross, A. 2014. *Creditocracy and the Case for Debt Refusal*. New York: OR Books.

Ryan, F. 2020. *Crippled: Austerity and the demonization of disabled people*. London: Verso Books.

Sepúlveda Carmona, M. 2013. *Report of the Special Rapporteur on Extreme Poverty and Human Rights: Unpaid care work and women's human rights*. Geneva: United Nations.

Shenaz Hossein, C. 2017. *The Black Social Economy in the Americas: Exploring diverse community-based markets*. New York: Springer.

Soederberg, S. 2005. 'The transnational debt architecture and emerging markets: The politics of paradoxes and punishment', *Third World Quarterly* 26 (6): 927–49.

Tronto, J. 1995. 'An ethic of care', *Generations: Journal of the American Society on Aging* 22 (3): 15–20.

Tronto, J. 2013. *Caring Democracy: Markets, equality, and justice*. New York: NYU Press.

United Nations. 2021. 'Secretary-General calls latest IPCC climate report "Code Red for Humanity", stressing "irrefutable" evidence of human influence'. Accessed 9 August 2021. https://www.un.org/press/en/2021/sgsm20847.doc.htm.

Wilkinson, R., and Pickett, K. 2010. *The Spirit Level: Why equality is better for everyone*. London: Penguin.

Index

suicides, rise in 6
Support for Mortgage Interest (SMI) benefit
    71n1
support systems, social networks as 123–5
Sustainable Development Goals, UN 127

tax reform (housing) 97–8
taxation 11, 92–3, 95, 152, 155, 159–60
temporary accommodation 24–5
Thatcher, Margaret 108–9
'there is no alternative' (TINA) 109
Tower Hamlets 142
'Tracey' bank note (HSCB) 104
Transparency International report (2013) 28
Treasury, HM 31, 76, 77, 96, 97
TUC (Trades Union Congress) 4
Turner, A. 72n3

UK State Investment Bank 96
unemployment 67, 76, 105
union membership 55
United States 22, 67, 81, 94
universal basic income 157
Universal Credit (UC) 5–6, 71n1, 118
unjust debts 44, 106, 112, 154–5, 160
unsecured credit/debt 4, 65, 67, 95
URBED (Urbanism Environment and Design)
    Ltd 143–4
utility
    arrears 13, 44, 117, 120
    costs 138–42

Voice4Change 126

wages 75, 152
    growth 61, 63, 94
Wealth and Assets Survey (WAS) 4
wealth funds 83
welfare, state 4, 61, 67–8, 116, 118, 157
    Universal Credit (UC) 5–6, 71n1, 118
Wimbledon Credit Union 49
Wolfe, Tom, The Bonfire of the Vanities 108
women 6, 157
working from home 91
Wren-Lewis, Simon 84
Wright, Christopher J. 37

young people 6

CPSIA information can be obtained
at www.ICGtesting.com
Printed in the USA
BVHW052236200323
660824BV00007B/19